STECK-VAUGHN
Level F

LANGUAGE

EXERCISES

FOR ADULTS

STECK-VAUGHN
COMPANY
ELEMENTARY • SECONDARY • ADULT • LIBRARY

Acknowledgments

Executive Editor: Diane Sharpe
Supervising Editor: Stephanie Muller
Project Editor: Patricia Claney
Design Manager: Laura Cole

Macmillan/McGraw-Hill School Publishing Company: Pronunciation Key,
reprinted with permission of the publisher, from *Macmillan School
Dictionary 1*. Copyright © 1990 Macmillan Publishing Company,
a division of Macmillan, Inc.

LANGUAGE EXERCISES Series:

Level A	Level D	Level G
Level B	Level E	Level H
Level C	Level F	Review

ISBN 0-8114-7880-7

Table of Contents

Unit 5 Composition

Unit 6 Study Skills

Final Reviews

A. Write S before each pair of synonyms, A before each pair of antonyms, and H before each pair of homonyms.

_____ **1.** full, empty   _____ **3.** journal, notebook

_____ **2.** lead, led   _____ **4.** would, wood

B. Write the homograph for the pair of meanings.

_____ **a.** a container   **b.** to be able

C. Write P before each word with a prefix, S before each word with a suffix, and C before each compound word.

_____ **1.** joyous   _____ **3.** disappear

_____ **2.** outcome   _____ **4.** mislead

D. Write the words that make up each contraction.

_____ _____ **1.** can't   _____ _____ **2.** they'll

E. Underline the word in parentheses that has the more positive connotation.

Our (nosy, curious) neighbor peeked over the fence.

F. Circle the letter of the idiom that means out of favor.

a. down in the dumps   **b.** in the doghouse

G. Write D before the declarative sentence, IM before the imperative sentence, E before the exclamatory sentence, and IN before the interrogative sentence. Then circle the simple subject, and underline the simple predicate in each sentence.

_____ **1.** Who is going with us?   _____ **3.** Don't worry about a thing.

_____ **2.** I feel awful!   _____ **4.** It is best to just wait.

H. Write CS before the sentence that has a compound subject. Write CP before the sentence that has a compound predicate.

_____ **1.** The dog growled and barked.

_____ **2.** Broccoli and carrots are tasty vegetables.

I. Write CS before the compound sentence. Write RO before the run-on sentence. Write I before the sentence that is in inverted order.

_____ **1.** We had been there once before, it was familiar to me.

_____ **2.** Around the corner sped the getaway car.

_____ **3.** Time was running out, and darkness was falling.

J. Underline the common nouns, and circle the proper nouns in the sentence.

The police officer told Paul that Judge Hawkins was the person who would decide.

K. **Write the correct possessive noun to complete the second sentence.**

The car of her friend was stolen. Her _____ car was stolen.

L. **Underline the appositive in the sentence. Circle the noun it identifies or explains.**

Nolan Ryan, a baseball star, is signing autographs at the store.

M. **Underline the verb phrase, and circle the helping verb.**

He will soon discover the error in his plan.

N. **Write past, present, or future to show the tense of each underlined verb.**

_____ **1.** Yesterday it rained very hard.

_____ **2.** Soon the clouds will disappear.

_____ **3.** Sunny days are my favorite.

O. **Circle the correct verbs in each sentence.**

1. Rosa (fly, flew) to Paris and (went, gone) to see the Eiffel Tower.

2. She (drink, drank) the soda and (throw, threw) the can in the recycling bin.

3. The ice (frozen, froze) hard but (broke, broken) up in the spring.

P. **Write SP before the sentence that has a subject pronoun, OP before the sentence that has an object pronoun, PP before the sentence that has a possessive pronoun, and IP before the sentence that has an indefinite pronoun. Circle the pronoun in each sentence.**

_____ **1.** You should take a nap.   _____ **3.** A smile was her answer.

_____ **2.** Nobody knew what happened.   _____ **4.** Frank didn't even hear us.

Q. **On the line before each sentence, write adjective or adverb to describe the underlined word.**

_____ **1.** These are my favorite books.

_____ **2.** He eats here regularly.

_____ **3.** You are too hasty.

_____ **4.** She is an actor.

R. **Circle the correct word in each sentence.**

1. (May, Can) you see from here?

2. You must (teach, learn) to be patient.

3. Just (sit, set) your shoes over there.

4. She (lied, laid) down the book.

5. He (doesn't, don't) want to go.

S. **Underline each prepositional phrase twice. Circle each preposition. Underline the conjunctions once.**

You can either wait in the car or outside the door.

T. Rewrite the letter. Use capital letters and punctuation marks where needed.

832 southern star
helena mt 95097
aug 27 1994

dear edward

    i have the information you wanted ____ did you ever think id get it to you this quickly ____ well its time i surprised you ____ heres what you should bring six cartons of orange juice forty five paper cups and three bags of ice ____ what a breakfast party this will be ____

your friend
bill

_____

_____

_____

_____

_____

_____

_____

_____

_____

_____

U. Write a topic sentence and two sentences with descriptive supporting details on the topic of home safety.

_____

_____

_____

V. Number the steps for writing a report in order.

_____ **1.** Write the report.
_____ **2.** Organize your research questions.
_____ **3.** Revise and proofread your report.
_____ **4.** Look in an encyclopedia.
_____ **5.** Write information in your own words.
_____ **6.** Make an outline.

W. Circle the part that does <u>not</u> belong in a business letter.

heading   closing   title   signature   body   greeting

X. Use the dictionary entry below to answer the questions.

carpet (kär′ pit) *n.* **1.** a thick floor covering; rug: *She cleaned the carpet.*
2. a surface like a rug: *A carpet of leaves covered the ground.*

1. What part of speech is the word <u>carpet</u>? _____

2. Would <u>carport</u> come before or after <u>carpet</u> in the dictionary? _____

3. Would <u>cart</u> / <u>cast</u> or <u>care</u> / <u>carrot</u> be the guide words for <u>carpet</u>? _____

4. Write the number of the definition for <u>carpet</u> in this sentence: The fawn lay on a carpet of grass. _____

5. Write the word for this respelling: (sûr′ fes) _____

6. Write <u>carpet</u> separated into syllables. _____

Y. Circle the information found on the title page of a book.

where a chapter begins   the author's name   the date the book was published

Z. Write the source from the box that you would use to find the information listed.

dictionary   card catalog   encyclopedia   atlas

_____ **1.** a map of the world

_____ **2.** an article on Africa

_____ **3.** how to pronounce a word

_____ **4.** to locate a book by Mark Twain

_____ **5.** information about recycled materials

Below is a list of the sections on *Check What You Know* and the pages on which the skills in each section are taught. If you missed any questions, turn to the pages listed, and practice the skills. Then correct the problems you missed on *Check What You Know*.

Synonyms and Antonyms

> ■ A **synonym** is a word that has the same or nearly the same meaning as one or more other words.   EXAMPLES: joy – happiness   choose – pick

A. Write a synonym for each word below.

1. small _____
2. swiftly _____
3. weary _____
4. pretty _____

5. large _____
6. awful _____
7. lad _____
8. forest _____

9. cry _____
10. leap _____
11. wealthy _____
12. ugly _____

B. Circle the word in parentheses that is a synonym for the underlined word in each sentence.

1. (finish, begin)   When you start to write, think about your audience.
2. (fall, spring)   The colors of autumn leaves are breathtaking.
3. (sick, well)   Last week I was ill with the flu.
4. (tried, tired)   He was exhausted after the marathon.
5. (clothes, close)   I tried to shut the door, but it was stuck.

> ■ An **antonym** is a word that has the opposite meaning of another word.
>   EXAMPLES: hot – cold   late – early

C. Write an antonym for each word below.

1. good _____
2. old _____
3. dull _____
4. thick _____

5. tall _____
6. crooked _____
7. happy _____
8. remember _____

9. ugly _____
10. near _____
11. obey _____
12. rich _____

D. Circle the word in parentheses that is an antonym for the underlined word in each sentence.

1. (heavy, hard)   The donkey strained under its light load.
2. (last, late)   The early morning sun streamed in the window.
3. (fine, kind)   Jerry gave the dog a mean pat on the head.
4. (empty, old)   I tried to pour some milk. but the carton was full.
5. (frowned, found)   Isabel lost her favorite book.

Lesson 2

Homonyms

■ A **homonym** is a word that sounds the same as another word but has a different spelling and a different meaning.
  EXAMPLES: to – two – too   sum – some

A. Underline the correct homonym(s) in each sentence below.

1. The couple walked for a mile along the (beech, beach).

2. Are there any (dear, deer) in these hills?

3. How much do you (way, weigh)?

4. Who broke this window (pane, pain)?

5. I have (to, too, two) go (to, too, two) the sale with those (to, too, two) people.

6. Laurie (knew, new) how to play a (new, knew) word game.

7. Juan and Luis spent a week at (there, their) friends' ranch.

8. Those boys (ate, eight) (ate, eight) of the apples we had just bought.

9. I like to walk by the (see, sea) at dusk.

10. (Wring, Ring) the bell, Matt.

11. Did you see what she brought (hear, here)?

12. He cannot (write, right) with his (write, right) hand.

13. Who has not (read, red) the magazine?

14. He found it cheaper to (buy, by) his pencils (buy, by) the box.

15. Chris told his niece a fairy (tale, tail).

B. Write a homonym for each word below.

1. hall _____	11. flower _____	21. our _____
2. threw _____	12. stair _____	22. sea _____
3. weak _____	13. pale _____	23. right _____
4. there _____	14. ring _____	24. peace _____
5. heard _____	15. soar _____	25. no _____
6. here _____	16. sale _____	26. grate _____
7. by _____	17. won _____	27. way _____
8. pane _____	18. aisle _____	28. cent _____
9. heal _____	19. rode _____	29. dew _____
10. blew _____	20. meet _____	30. forth _____

Lesson 3 — Homographs

■ A **homograph** is a word that has the same spelling as another word but a different meaning and sometimes a different pronunciation.
EXAMPLE: <u>bow</u>, meaning "to bend the upper part of the body forward in respect," and <u>bow</u>, meaning "a weapon for shooting arrows"

vault	checks	interest

A. Fill in each blank with a homograph from the box. Use each homograph twice.

1. With a bank account, you can write _____ to pay for things.

2. She looked with great _____ at the painting.

3. He used a long pole to _____ over the jump.

4. My savings account pays _____ on the money I keep in it.

5. José keeps his stamp collection locked in a _____ .

6. She wrote small _____ beside each item on the list.

B. Circle the letter of the correct definition for each underlined homograph. Then write a sentence using the other meaning of the homograph.

1. Put your coins in the <u>bank</u>.

   a. a place where people save money   **b.** the ground along a river

   _____

2. If you <u>hide</u> your bank, be sure to remember where you put it.

   a. keep out of sight   **b.** the skin of an animal

   _____

3. Some people keep their money in a <u>safe</u>.

   a. a metal box with a lock   **b.** free from danger

   _____

4. There are only two people who have the <u>key</u> to open the safe.

   a. a piece of metal to open a lock   **b.** a low island or reef

   _____

5. Many people have an <u>account</u> at a bank.

   a. explanation   **b.** an amount of money

   _____

> ■ A **prefix** added to the beginning of a base word changes the meaning of the word.
>   EXAMPLE: <u>un-</u>, meaning "not," + the base word <u>done</u> = <u>undone</u>, meaning "not done"
> ■ Some prefixes have one meaning, and others have more than one meaning.
>
> | EXAMPLES: | **prefix** | **meaning** |
> |---|---|---|
> | | im-, in-, non-, un- | not |
> | | dis-, in-, non- | opposite of, lack of, not |
> | | mis- | bad, badly, wrong, wrongly |
> | | pre- | before |
> | | re- | again |

A. Add the prefix <u>un-</u>, <u>im-</u>, <u>non-</u>, or <u>mis-</u> to the base word in parentheses. Write the new word in the sentence. Then write the definition of the new word on the line after the sentence. Use a dictionary if necessary.

1. It is _____ (practical) to put a new monkey into a cage with other monkeys.

   _____

2. The monkeys might _____ (behave) with a newcomer among them.

   _____

3. They will also feel quite _____ (easy) for a number of days or even weeks.

   _____

4. Even if the new monkey is _____ (violent) in nature, the others may harm it.

   _____

5. Sometimes animal behavior can be quite _____ (usual).

   _____

B. Underline each prefix. Write the meaning of each word that has a prefix.

1. unexpected guest _____

2. really disappear _____

3. disagree often _____

4. misspell a name _____

5. preview a movie _____

6. reenter a room _____

7. misplace a shoe _____

8. impossible situation _____

9. nonstop reading _____

10. unimportant discussion _____

11. insane story _____

12. prejudge a person _____

Lesson 5 — Suffixes

> ■ A **suffix** added to the end of a base word changes the meaning of the word.
>   EXAMPLE: -ful, meaning "full of," + the base word <u>joy</u> = <u>joyful</u>,
>   meaning "full of joy"
> ■ Some suffixes have one meaning, and others have more than one meaning.
>   EXAMPLES:
>
> | suffix | meaning |
> |--------|---------|
> | -able | able to be, suitable or inclined to |
> | -al | relating to, like |
> | -ful | as much as will fill, full of |
> | -less | without, that does not |
> | -ous | full of |
> | -y | having, full of |

A. Add a suffix from the list above to the base word in parentheses. Write the new word. Then write the definition of the new word on the line after the sentence. Do not use any suffix more than once.

1. Switzerland is a _____ country. (mountain)

   _____

2. If you visit there, it is _____ to have a walking stick. (help)

   _____

3. Many tourists visit the country's _____ mountains to ski each year. (snow)

   _____

4. The Swiss people have a great deal of _____ pride. (nation)

   _____

5. Many Swiss are _____ about several languages. (knowledge)

   _____

B. Underline each suffix. Write the meaning of each word that has a suffix.

1. breakable toy _____

2. endless waves _____

3. hazardous path _____

4. inflatable raft _____

5. poisonous snake _____

6. dependable trains _____

7. humorous program _____

8. tearful goodbye _____

9. bumpy ride _____

10. careless driver _____

11. natural food _____

12. magical wand _____

> ■ A **contraction** is a word formed by joining two other words.
> ■ An **apostrophe** shows where a letter or letters have been left out.   EXAMPLE: do not = don't
> ■ <u>Won't</u> is an exception.   EXAMPLE: will not = won't

A. **Underline each contraction. Write the words that make up each contraction on the line.**

1. Stingrays look as if they're part bird, part fish. _____

2. Stingrays cover themselves with sand so they won't be seen. _____

3. There's a chance that waders might step on a stingray and get stung. _____

4. That's a painful way to learn that you shouldn't forget about stingrays.

    _____   _____

5. Until recently, stingrays weren't seen very often. _____

6. It doesn't seem likely, but some stingrays will eat out of divers' hands. _____

7. Because its mouth is underneath, the stingray can't see what it's eating.

    _____   _____

8. Once they've been fed by hand, they'll flutter around for more.

    _____   _____

9. It's hard to believe these stingrays aren't afraid of humans.

    _____   _____

10. To pet a stingray, they'd gently touch its velvety skin. _____

B. **Find the pairs of words that can be made into contractions. Underline each pair. Then write the contraction each word pair can make on the lines following the sentences.**

1. I have never tried scuba diving, but I would like to.

    _____   _____

2. It is a good way to explore what is under the water.

    _____   _____

3. First, I will need to take lessons in the pool. _____

4. Then I can find out what to do if the equipment does not work. _____

Lesson 7

Compound Words

> ■ A **compound word** is a word that is made up of two or more words. The meaning of a compound word is related to the meaning of each individual word.
>   EXAMPLE: sun + glasses = sunglasses, meaning "glasses to wear in the sun"
> ■ Compound words may be written as one word, as hyphenated words, or as two separate words.
>   EXAMPLES: highway   high-rise   high school

A. Answer the following questions.

1. Something that has sharp, curved points extending backward is said to be barbed.

   What is barbed wire? _____

2. Dry means "without water." What does dry-clean mean? _____

3. Head means "a heading." What is a headline? _____

4. A deputy is "a person appointed to take the place of another."

   What is a deputy marshal? _____

5. Bare means "without a covering." What does bareback mean? _____

6. A road is a route. What is a railroad? _____

7. A paper is a type of document. What is a newspaper? _____

8. Blue is a color. What is a blueberry? _____

B. Combine words from the box to make compound words. Use the compound words to complete the sentences. You will use one word twice.

cut	every	fore	hair	head	where
loud	news	speaker	stand	thing	

1. Bob's hair covered his _____.

2. He knew it was time to get a _____.

3. He saw a truck hit a fire hydrant, which sprayed water _____.

4. The corner _____ was soaked.

5. A police officer used a _____ to direct traffic.

6. It was so exciting, Bob forgot about _____, including his haircut!

Connotation/Denotation

> ■ The **denotation** of a word is its exact meaning as stated in a dictionary.
>   EXAMPLE: The denotation of skinny is "very thin."
> ■ The **connotation** of a word is an added meaning that suggests
>   something positive or negative.
>   EXAMPLES: **Negative:** Skinny suggests "too thin." Skinny has
>   a negative connotation.
>   **Positive:** Slender suggests "attractively thin." Slender has
>   a positive connotation.
> ■ Some words are neutral. They do not suggest either good or bad feelings.
>   EXAMPLES: month, building, chair

A. Underline the word in parentheses that has the more positive connotation.

1. Our trip to the amusement park was (fine, wonderful).

2. (Brave, Foolhardy) people rode on the roller coaster.

3. We saw (fascinating, weird) animals in the animal house.

4. Some of the monkeys made (hilarious, amusing) faces.

5. Everyone had a (smile, smirk) on his or her face on the way home.

B. Underline the word in parentheses that has the more negative connotation.

1. We bought (cheap, inexpensive) souvenirs at the amusement park.

2. I ate a (soggy, moist) sandwich.

3. Mike (nagged, reminded) us to go to the funny house.

4. The funny house was (comical, silly).

5. I didn't like the (smirk, grin) on the jester's face.

6. It made me feel (uneasy, frightened).

C. Answer the following questions.

1. Which is worth more, something old or something antique? _____

2. Is it better to be slender or to be skinny? _____

3. Which would you rather be called, thrifty or cheap? _____

4. Would a vain person be more likely to stroll or to parade? _____

5. Which is more serious, a problem or a disaster? _____

6. Is it more polite to sip a drink or to gulp it? _____

7. If you hadn't eaten for weeks, would you be hungry or starving? _____

8. After walking in mud, would your shoes be dirty or filthy? _____

> ■ An **idiom** is an expression that has a meaning different from the usual
> meanings of the individual words within it.
>   EXAMPLE: <u>To lend a hand</u> means "to help," not "to loan someone a hand."

A. Match the idioms underlined in the sentences below with their meanings. Write the correct letter on each line.

a. in a risky situation

b. do less than I should

c. admit having said the wrong thing

d. play music after only hearing it

e. spend money carefully

f. continue to have hope

g. listen with all your attention

h. teasing

i. accept defeat

j. meet by chance

_____ **1.** I had hoped to <u>run across</u> some old friends at the ball game.

_____ **2.** Their team was ready to <u>throw in the towel</u> when we scored our tenth run!

_____ **3.** Peggy was <u>pulling my leg</u> when she told me that there are koala bears in Africa.

_____ **4.** I told her that she was <u>skating on thin ice</u> when she tried to trick me.

_____ **5.** My sister must <u>make ends meet</u> with the little money she has for college.

_____ **6.** I told her, "Always <u>keep your chin up</u> when things get difficult."

_____ **7.** José can <u>play by ear</u> the theme songs to all his favorite movies.

_____ **8.** If you don't believe me, just <u>be all ears</u> when he plays.

_____ **9.** My brother said that I would <u>lie down on the job</u> if he weren't watching over me.

_____ **10.** I told Bill that he would <u>eat his words</u> once he saw how much work I had done.

B. Underline the idioms in the following sentences. On the line after each sentence, explain what the idiom means. Use a dictionary if necessary.

1. Frank was in hot water when he arrived late.

_____

2. His friends were beside themselves with worry.

_____

3. Frank told them not to fly off the handle.

_____

4. His friends explained that they had been shaken up.

_____

5. They all decided to sit down and talk turkey.

_____

A. Write a synonym and an antonym for each underlined word below.

1. a <u>pleasant</u> trip _____ _____

2. to <u>increase</u> speed _____ _____

3. an <u>awful</u> mistake _____ _____

4. a <u>funny</u> joke _____ _____

5. a <u>correct</u> answer _____ _____

6. a <u>dangerous</u> stunt _____ _____

B. Underline the correct homonyms in each sentence below.

1. If you go by (plane, plain), you'll arrive (there, their) more quickly than by bus.

2. A bus could take a (weak, week), but you'll get (to, too, two) (see, sea) more.

3. If you couldn't (bear, bare) a long trip, an overnight trip (wood, would) do instead.

4. An overnight trip can be (cheep, cheap), relaxing, and a nice (break, brake) in your busy (week, weak).

C. Circle the letter of the correct definition for each underlined homograph. Then write a sentence using the other meaning of the homograph.

1. If you like to feel the <u>wind</u> in your hair, you might like sailing.

   a. moving air   **b.** to wrap in a circle

   _____

2. A sailboat will often <u>heel</u> if the sails are tight and the winds are strong.

   a. the rounded back part of the foot   **b.** lean to one side

   _____

3. It should only take a <u>minute</u> to complete the survey.

   a. a time period of sixty seconds   **b.** extremely small

   _____

4. Our city has had a <u>rash</u> of burglaries in the last two weeks.

   a. a skin problem   **b.** an outbreak of incidents within a short time period

   _____

D. Underline the prefix in each phrase below. Then write the meaning of each word that has the prefix.

1. impossible problem _____

2. incomplete work _____

3. uneasy feeling _____

4. nonviolent protest _____

5. disinterested student _____

6. refurnish a house _____

7. mispronounce a word _____

8. prehistoric animal _____

E. Underline the suffix in each phrase below. Then write the meaning of each word that has the suffix.

1. hazardous road _____

2. helpless kitten _____

3. profitable business _____

4. regional finals _____

F. Write the contraction each word pair can make.

1. we will _____

2. she would _____

3. will not _____

4. they have _____

5. you will _____

6. we are _____

G. Combine words from the box to make compound words. Use the compound words to complete the sentences.

road	table	sand	snow	plow	cross	lot	top

1. When we came to the _____ , we turned right.

2. The children played football in the _____ .

3. Tim needed a _____ to clear the road to the highway.

4. The family photograph on the _____ was nicely framed.

H. For each pair of phrases below, write the underlined word that has a positive connotation.

_____ 1. **a.** cheap material   **b.** inexpensive material

_____ 2. **a.** cozy apartment   **b.** cramped apartment

_____ 3. **a.** curious neighbor   **b.** nosy neighbor

_____ 4. **a.** lazy dog   **b.** relaxed dog

I. Underline the idiom in each of the following sentences. On the line after the sentence, explain what the idiom means.

1. You should stay on your toes while driving a car.

_____

2. If you run across a friend, stop and talk.

_____

3. Eileen saw red when she noticed graffiti on her new fence.

_____

4. When Sarah gave her speech, the audience was all ears.

_____

A. Rewrite the following sentences, using synonyms for the underlined words.

1. The lightning flashed across the <u>black</u> sky as the trees <u>bent</u> in the wind.

_____

2. <u>Blasts</u> of wind whistled through the <u>openings</u> between the boards on the window.

_____

3. Then a <u>hush</u> seemed to fall over our part of the <u>world</u>.

_____

B. Rewrite the following sentences, using antonyms for the underlined words.

1. <u>Before</u> the storm hit, the sky got <u>darker</u>.

_____

2. <u>Black</u> clouds drifted across the <u>evening</u> sky.

_____

3. The <u>heavy</u> wind was blowing leaves <u>over</u> the trees.

_____

C. Write a sentence using a homonym for each word.

1. new _____

2. grater _____

3. choose _____

4. weight _____

5. waist _____

D. For each homograph below, write two sentences. Be sure to use a different meaning of the homograph in each sentence.

1. light   a. _____

          b. _____

2. shed   a. _____

          b. _____

3. rest   a. _____

          b. _____

E. Add one of the following prefixes or suffixes to each base word to make a new word.

> **Prefixes:** in-, non-, dis-, mis-, pre-, re-
> **Suffixes:** -able, -ful, -less

1. place _____

2. direct _____

3. use _____

4. measure _____

5. speech _____

6. tire _____

7. remark _____

8. spell _____

9. pay _____

10. fund _____

F. Use the following idioms in sentences. Use a dictionary if necessary.

1. throw in the towel _____

2. pulling my leg _____

3. skating on thin ice _____

4. get in touch with _____

5. keep an eye on _____

G. Think of words that have almost the same meaning as the neutral word, but have a more negative or positive connotation. Complete the chart with your words.

Negative Connotation	Neutral	Positive Connotation
1. _____	wet	_____
2. _____	shout	_____
3. _____	thin	_____
4. _____	old	_____
5. _____	talk	_____
6. _____	clothes	_____
7. _____	ask	_____
8. _____	work	_____
9. _____	cut	_____
10. _____	eat	_____

> ■ A **sentence** is a group of words that expresses a complete thought.
> EXAMPLE: Marie sings well.

■ **Some of the following groups of words are sentences, and some are not. Write <u>S</u> before each group that is a sentence. Punctuate each sentence with a period.**

_____ **1.** When the downhill skiing season begins____

_____ **2.** Last summer I visited my friend in New Jersey____

_____ **3.** From the very beginning of the first-aid lessons____

_____ **4.** One of the children from the neighborhood____

_____ **5.** A visiting musician played the organ____

_____ **6.** On the way to school this morning____

_____ **7.** "I love you, Mother," said Mike____

_____ **8.** The blue house at the corner of Maple Street____

_____ **9.** After Emily left, the phone rang off the hook____

_____ **10.** Speak distinctly and loudly so that you can be heard____

_____ **11.** I have finally learned to drive our car____

_____ **12.** This is William's tenth birthday____

_____ **13.** At the very last moment, we were ready____

_____ **14.** When you speak in front of people____

_____ **15.** The basket of fruit on the table____

_____ **16.** Please answer the telephone, Julia____

_____ **17.** Hurrying to class because he is late____

_____ **18.** The first thing in the morning____

_____ **19.** That mistake was costly and unfortunate____

_____ **20.** We are planning to build a new doghouse____

_____ **21.** The dog chased the cat up the tree____

_____ **22.** Daniel Boone was born in Pennsylvania____

_____ **23.** The giant cottonwood in our backyard____

_____ **24.** Marla, bring my notebook____

_____ **25.** On a stool beside the back door____

_____ **26.** Sometimes the noise from the street____

_____ **27.** Somewhere out of state____

_____ **28.** The band played a lively march____

_____ **29.** That flight arrived on time____

_____ **30.** Was cracked in dozens of places____

Lesson 11 — Types of Sentences

> - A **declarative** sentence makes a statement. It is followed by a period (.).   EXAMPLES: It is warm today. I took off my coat.
> - An **interrogative** sentence asks a question. It is followed by a question mark (?).   EXAMPLES: When is Tony coming? Why is the bus late today?

- **Write D before each declarative sentence and IN before each interrogative sentence. Put the correct punctuation mark at the end of the sentence.**

IN   **1.** Who is your favorite author ?

_____ **2.** How are our forests protected from fire ___

_____ **3.** Tim learned the names of the trees in his neighborhood ___

_____ **4.** A good driver obeys every traffic law ___

_____ **5.** The hippopotamus lives in Africa ___

_____ **6.** Do you know the legend of the dogwood tree ___

_____ **7.** Every sentence should begin with a capital letter ___

_____ **8.** Ryan is repairing the lamp ___

_____ **9.** Did you ever see a kangaroo ___

_____ **10.** Where did these fragrant roses grow ___

_____ **11.** Beautiful furniture can be made from the oak tree ___

_____ **12.** Flour can be made from dried bananas ___

_____ **13.** Did anyone find Steve's book ___

_____ **14.** Andrea feeds the goldfish every day ___

_____ **15.** How many people are studying to be pilots ___

_____ **16.** Kelly is going to the show with us ___

_____ **17.** Last summer we made a trip to Carlsbad Caverns ___

_____ **18.** How old are you ___

_____ **19.** The architect and her assistant inspected the building ___

_____ **20.** When did you arrive at the meeting ___

_____ **21.** Did you forget your wallet ___

_____ **22.** That light bulb is burned out ___

_____ **23.** The baby crawled across the room ___

_____ **24.** When would you like to eat ___

_____ **25.** Jo helped Andy wash the car ___

_____ **26.** Did they wax the car ___

_____ **27.** How did you make that sand castle ___

_____ **28.** It is easy to make if we work together ___

More Types of Sentences

> - An **imperative** sentence expresses a command or a request. It is followed by a period (.). EXAMPLE: Close the door.
> - An **exclamatory** sentence expresses strong or sudden feeling. It is followed by an exclamation point (!). EXAMPLE: I am innocent!

- **Write IM before each imperative sentence and E before each exclamatory sentence. Put the correct punctuation mark at the end of each sentence.**

IM   **1.** Write the names of the days of the week.

_____ **2.** Please mail this package for me___

_____ **3.** I love the gift you gave me___

_____ **4.** Lay the papers on the desk___

_____ **5.** How beautiful the night is___

_____ **6.** Watch out for that turning car___

_____ **7.** Drive more slowly___

_____ **8.** Keep time with the music___

_____ **9.** Deliver this message immediately___

_____ **10.** Sign your name in my yearbook___

_____ **11.** That airplane is so huge___

_____ **12.** Please lend me a postage stamp___

_____ **13.** I'm delighted with the flowers___

_____ **14.** How blue the sky is___

_____ **15.** My neighbor's shed is on fire___

_____ **16.** The baby's lip is bleeding___

_____ **17.** I can't believe that I got a perfect score___

_____ **18.** Pass the green beans___

_____ **19.** Write down these sentences___

_____ **20.** That movie was so exciting___

_____ **21.** The puppy is so playful___

_____ **22.** Look both ways when crossing the street___

_____ **23.** What a pretty red and blue sailboat___

_____ **24.** Please repeat what you said___

_____ **25.** Put the vase on the table___

_____ **26.** Be more careful with your work___

_____ **27.** That's a fantastic book to read___

_____ **28.** This is a wonderful surprise___

> ■ Every sentence has two main parts, a **complete subject** and a **complete predicate**.
> ■ The complete subject includes all the words that tell who or what the sentence is about.
> EXAMPLES: **My brother**/likes to go with us. **Six geese**/honked loudly.
> ■ The complete predicate includes all the words that state the action or condition of the subject.
> EXAMPLES: My brother/**likes to go with us**. Six geese/**honked loudly**.

■ **Draw a line between the complete subject and the complete predicate in each sentence.**

1. Bees/fly.

2. Trains whistle.

3. A talented artist drew this cartoon.

4. The wind blew furiously.

5. My grandmother made this dress last year.

6. We surely have enjoyed the holiday.

7. These cookies are made with rice.

8. This letter came to the post office box.

9. They rent a cabin in Colorado every summer.

10. Jennifer is reading about the pioneer days in the West.

11. Our baseball team won the third game of the series.

12. The band played a cheerful tune.

13. A cloudless sky is a great help to a pilot.

14. The voice of the auctioneer was heard throughout the hall.

15. A sudden flash of lightning startled us.

16. The wind howled down the chimney.

17. Paul's dog followed him to the grocery store.

18. Their apartment is on the sixth floor.

19. We have studied many interesting places.

20. Each player on the team deserves credit for the victory.

21. Forest rangers fought the raging fire.

22. A friend taught Robert a valuable lesson.

23. Millions of stars make up the Milky Way.

24. The airplane was lost in the thick clouds.

25. Many of the children waded in the pool.

26. Yellowstone Park is a large national park.

27. Cold weather is predicted for tomorrow.

28. The trees were covered with moss.

Lesson 14

Simple Subjects and Predicates

> - The **simple subject** of a sentence is the main word in the complete subject. The simple subject is a noun or a word that stands for a noun.
>   EXAMPLE: My **sister**/lost her gloves.
> - Sometimes the simple subject is also the complete subject.
>   EXAMPLE: **She**/lost her gloves.
> - The **simple predicate** of a sentence is a verb within the complete predicate. The simple predicate may be a one-word verb or a verb of more than one word.
>   EXAMPLES: She/**lost** her gloves. She/**is looking** for them.

- **Draw a line between the complete subject and complete predicate in each sentence below. Underline the simple subject once and the simple predicate twice.**

1. A sudden <u>clap</u> of thunder/<u>frightened</u> all of us.

2. The soft snow covered the fields and roads.

3. We drove very slowly over the narrow bridge.

4. The students are making an aquarium.

5. Our class read about the founder of Hull House.

6. The women were talking in the park.

7. This album has many folk songs.

8. We are furnishing the sandwiches for tonight's picnic.

9. All the trees on that lawn are giant oaks.

10. Many Americans are working in foreign countries.

11. The manager read the names of the contest winners.

12. Bill brought these large melons.

13. We opened the front door of the house.

14. The two mechanics worked on the car for an hour.

15. Black and yellow butterflies fluttered among the flowers.

16. The child spoke politely.

17. We found many beautiful shells along the shore.

18. The best part of the program is the dance number.

19. Every ambitious person is working hard.

20. Sheryl swam across the lake two times.

21. Our program will begin promptly at eight o'clock.

22. The handle of this basket is broken.

23. The clock in the tower strikes every hour.

24. The white farmhouse on that road belongs to my cousin.

25. The first game of the season will be played tomorrow.

Subjects and Predicates in Inverted Order

> - When the subject of a sentence comes before all or part of the predicate, the sentence is in **natural order.**
>   EXAMPLE: The puppy scampered away.
> - When all or part of the predicate comes before the subject, the sentence is in **inverted order.**
>   EXAMPLE: Away scampered the puppy.
> - Many interrogative sentences are in inverted order.
>   EXAMPLE: Where is/James?

A. Draw a line between the complete subject and the complete predicate in each sentence. Write I in front of sentences that are in inverted order.

___I___ 1. Lightly falls/the mist.

_____ 2. The peaches on this tree are ripe now.

_____ 3. Over and over rolled the rocks.

_____ 4. Down the street marched the band.

_____ 5. Near the ocean are many birds.

_____ 6. Right under the chair ran the kitten.

_____ 7. He hit the ball a long way.

_____ 8. Along the ridge hiked the campers.

_____ 9. Underground is the stream.

_____ 10. The fish jumped in the lake.

_____ 11. Over the hill came the trucks.

_____ 12. Out came the rainbow.

B. Rewrite each inverted sentence in Exercise A in natural order.

1. _____

2. _____

3. _____

4. _____

5. _____

6. _____

7. _____

8. _____

9. _____

Using Compound Subjects

> ■ Two sentences in which the subjects are different but the predicates are the same can be combined into one sentence. The two subjects are joined by <u>and</u>. The subject of the new sentence is called a **compound subject.**
>
> EXAMPLE: **Lynn** visited an amusement park.
> **Eric** visited an amusement park.
> **Lynn and Eric** visited an amusement park.

A. Draw a line between the complete subject and the complete predicate in each sentence. If the subject is compound, write <u>CS</u> before the sentence.

___CS___ **1.** English settlers and Spanish settlers/came to North America in the 1600s.

_____ **2.** Trees and bushes were chopped down to make room for their houses.

_____ **3.** The fierce winds and the cold temperatures made the first winters very harsh.

_____ **4.** The settlers and Native Americans became friends.

_____ **5.** Native Americans helped the settlers grow food in the new country.

_____ **6.** Potatoes and corn were first grown by Native Americans.

_____ **7.** English settlers and Spanish settlers had never tasted turkey.

_____ **8.** Peanuts and sunflower seeds are Native American foods that we now eat for snacks.

_____ **9.** Lima beans and corn are combined to make succotash.

_____ **10.** Zucchini is an American squash that was renamed by Italian settlers.

_____ **11.** Native Americans also introduced barbecuing to the settlers.

B. Combine each pair of sentences below. Underline the compound subject.

1. Gold from the New World was sent to Spain. Silver from the New World was sent to Spain.

_____

_____

2. France staked claims in the Americas in the 1500s and 1600s. The Netherlands staked claims in the Americas in the 1500s and 1600s.

_____

_____

3. John Cabot explored areas of the Americas. Henry Hudson explored areas of the Americas.

_____

_____

C. Write a sentence with a compound subject.

_____

_____

Lesson 17

Using Compound Predicates

> ■ Two sentences in which the subjects are the same but the predicates are different can be combined into one sentence. The two predicates may be joined by <u>or</u>, <u>and</u>, or <u>but</u>. The predicate of the new sentence is called a **compound predicate.**
>
> EXAMPLE: The crowd **cheered** the players.
> The crowd **applauded** the players.
> The crowd **cheered and applauded** the players.

A. Draw a line between the complete subject and the complete predicate in each sentence. If the predicate is compound, write <u>CP</u> before the sentence.

_____ 1. The students organized a picnic for their families.

_____ 2. They discussed and chose a date for the picnic.

_____ 3. They wrote and designed invitations.

_____ 4. The invitations were mailed and delivered promptly.

_____ 5. Twenty-five families responded to the invitations.

_____ 6. The students bought the food and made the sandwiches.

_____ 7. The families bought the soft drinks.

_____ 8. The students packed and loaded the food into a truck.

_____ 9. The families brought and set up the volleyball nets.

_____ 10. Everyone participated in the games and races.

_____ 11. They ran relay races and threw water balloons.

_____ 12. Everyone packed the food and cleaned up the picnic area at the end of the day.

B. Combine each pair of sentences below. Underline the compound predicate.

1. Caroline heard the music. Caroline memorized the music.

_____

_____

2. Keith picked up the newspapers. Keith loaded the newspapers into his car.

_____

_____

3. Larry studied the names of the states. Larry wrote down the names of the states.

_____

_____

C. Write a sentence with a compound predicate.

_____

Simple and Compound Sentences

- A **simple sentence** has one subject and one predicate.
  EXAMPLE: The earth/is covered by land and water.
- A **compound sentence** is made up of two simple sentences joined by a connecting word such as <u>and</u>, <u>but</u>, and <u>or</u>. A comma is placed before the connecting word.
  EXAMPLE: One-fourth of the earth/is covered by land, and the land/is divided into seven continents.

A. Draw a line between the complete subject and the complete predicate in each sentence. Write <u>S</u> before each simple sentence. Write <u>C</u> before each compound sentence.

_____ 1. The seven continents of the world are North America, South America, Africa, Europe, Australia, Asia, and Antarctica.

_____ 2. Three-fourths of the earth is covered by water, and most of it is salty ocean water.

_____ 3. The four oceans of the world are the Pacific, the Atlantic, the Indian, and the Arctic.

_____ 4. We cannot exist without water, but we cannot drink the salty ocean water.

_____ 5. Most of the water we drink comes from lakes, rivers, and streams.

_____ 6. Clean water is a priceless resource.

B. Combine each pair of simple sentences below into a compound sentence.

1. The Pacific Ocean is the largest ocean in the world.
   It covers more area than all the earth's land put together.

   _____

   _____

2. Bodies of saltwater that are smaller than oceans are called seas, gulfs, or bays.
   These bodies of water are often encircled by land.

   _____

   _____

3. Seas, gulfs, and bays are joined to the oceans.
   They vary in size and depth.

   _____

   _____

4. The Mediterranean is one of the earth's largest seas.
   It is almost entirely encircled by the southern part of Europe, the northern part of Africa, and the western part of Asia.

   _____

   _____

   _____

Lesson
19

Correcting Run-on Sentences

> ■ Two or more sentences run together without the correct punctuation are called a **run-on sentence.**
>   EXAMPLE: It will rain today, it will be sunny tomorrow.
> ■ One way to correct a run-on sentence is to separate it into two sentences.
>   EXAMPLE: It will rain today. It will be sunny tomorrow.
> ■ Another way to correct a run-on sentence is to separate the two main parts with a comma and <u>and</u>, <u>or</u>, <u>but</u>, <u>nor</u>, or <u>yet</u>.
>   EXAMPLE: It will rain today, but it will be sunny tomorrow.

■ **Rewrite each run-on sentence correctly.**

1. In 1860, the Pony Express started in St. Joseph, Missouri the route began where the railroads ended.

   _____

   _____

2. People in the West wanted faster mail service, the mail took six weeks by boat.

   _____

   _____

3. Mail sent by stagecoach took about 21 days, the Pony Express averaged ten days.

   _____

   _____

4. The Pony Express used a relay system riders and horses were switched at 157 places along the way to Sacramento, California.

   _____

   _____

5. Because teenagers weighed less than adults, most of the riders were teenagers the horses could run faster carrying them.

   _____

   _____

6. Riders had to cross raging rivers, the mountains were another barrier.

   _____

   _____

Expanding Sentences

Unit 2, Sentences

- Sentences can be **expanded** by adding details to make them clearer and more interesting.
    EXAMPLE: The child waved. The child **in the blue hat** waved **timidly to me.**
- Details added to sentences may answer these questions: When? (today) Where? (at home) How? (slowly) How often? (daily) To what degree? (very) What kind? (big) Which? (smallest) How many? (five)

A. Expand each sentence by adding details to answer the questions shown in parentheses. Write the expanded sentence on the line.

1. The ball soared.   (What kind? Where?)

_____

2. It crashed.   (How? Where?)

_____

3. It rolled.   (When? Where?)

_____

4. I felt.   (How? To what degree?)

_____

B. Decide how each of the following sentences can be expanded. Write your new sentence on the line.

1. The fires spread. _____

_____

2. People ran. _____

_____

3. Homes and trees blazed. _____

_____

4. Firefighters came. _____

_____

5. Water sprayed. _____

_____

6. Flames died out. _____

_____

A. Label each sentence as follows: Write **D** if it is declarative, **IN** if it is interrogative, **IM** if it is imperative, and **E** if it is exclamatory. Write **X** if the group of words is not a sentence. Punctuate each sentence correctly.

_____ **1.** What is your favorite radio station ____

_____ **2.** The one I listen to is having a contest ____

_____ **3.** Call this number to win a prize ____

_____ **4.** If you are the seventh caller ____

_____ **5.** The winner will be announced immediately ____

_____ **6.** I just won ____

_____ **7.** What did I win ____

_____ **8.** A trip to the Bahamas ____

_____ **9.** I'm so excited ____

_____ **10.** Who wants to go with me ____

B. Draw a line between the complete subject and the complete predicate in each sentence below. Underline the simple subject once. Underline the simple predicate twice.

1. You must guess the number of beans in the jar.

2. John will write his guesses on these pieces of paper.

3. His younger sister has already written her guess.

4. His twin brothers will write their guesses after school.

5. Each member of the family hopes to guess the winning number.

6. Only one person can win.

C. The sentences below are in inverted order. Rewrite each sentence in natural order.

1. In the mail came Maria's contest entry form. _____

_____

2. Right into the trash went her contestant prize number. _____

_____

3. In the city dump was buried the winning prize number. _____

_____

4. What she did Maria will never know. _____

_____

D. Label each sentence below as follows: Write <u>CS</u> if it has a compound subject, <u>CP</u> if it has a compound predicate, <u>C</u> if it is a compound sentence, and <u>R</u> if it is a run-on sentence.

_____ **1.** Contestants buy something and fill out a form.

_____ **2.** Rules and dates for a contest are often printed on the entry form.

_____ **3.** Some contests require contestants to create something some do not.

_____ **4.** I think of contests as challenging, and I often enter them.

_____ **5.** My brother and I created a jingle for one interesting contest.

_____ **6.** I wrote the words for the jingle, and my brother wrote the music.

_____ **7.** We made a tape of our jingle and mailed it in.

_____ **8.** Our jingle was the winning entry we were so excited.

E. Combine each pair of sentences below. Underline the compound subject or compound predicate.

1. Jan listened to the song playing on the radio. Paul listened to the song playing on the radio. _____

_____

2. They both knew the title of the song. They both remembered who recorded it. _____

_____

F. Combine each pair of simple sentences to make a compound sentence.

1. I enjoy entering recipe contests. My favorite contests are for dessert recipes. _____

_____

2. I create most of my recipes from scratch. I add unusual ingredients to existing recipes. _____

_____

G. Rewrite each run-on sentence correctly.

1. Many people win contests every day some people just have to write their names on an entry form to win.

_____

2. Some contest winners are given numbers, the winning prize numbers are drawn randomly. _____

_____

H. Expand the sentence below by inserting details. Write your expanded sentence on the blank lines.

1. The contest was won by a woman. _____

_____

A. Write complete sentences with each group of words below. In each sentence, underline the simple subject once and the simple predicate twice.

1. when I speak in front of people

_____

2. the noise from the street

_____

3. on the way to school this morning

_____

4. a long way from home

_____

5. had a birthday party for Diane

_____

B. Complete each sentence below to make the kind of sentence named. Be sure to use the correct end punctuation.

1. Declarative   The solar system consists of _____

2. Interrogative   Which is the largest _____

3. Imperative   Tell the class _____

4. Exclamatory   What an enormous _____

C. To each compound subject or compound predicate below, add whatever words are needed to make a sentence.

1. _____ arrived at the game and sat in their seats.

2. _____ swept the plate and cried, "Play ball!"

3. The batter and the pitcher _____.

4. _____ swung at and missed the ball.

5. The pitcher and the catcher _____.

6. _____ hit the ball and ran the bases.

D. Write two sentences in inverted order.

_____

_____

E. Rewrite the sentences below, making one of these improvements: (a) combine sentences by using compound subjects or compound predicates; (b) combine simple sentences to make compound sentences; (c) correct run-on sentences.

1. To take a good photograph, you need a good eye you do not need an expensive camera.

_____

_____

2. You just load your camera then you go for a walk.

_____

3. You may see something that is different. You may see something that is colorful.

_____

_____

4. Perhaps you like the shape of an object or maybe you like the texture of an object.

_____

_____

5. Don't take your picture yet be sure your lens cap is off and your camera is focused correctly.

_____

_____

6. Think about what you do not want in your picture. Think about the way you want to frame your picture.

_____

_____

7. Take your time. Keep your camera steady.

_____

_____

F. Expand each sentence below by adding details that make it clearer and more interesting.

1. The traffic roars on the highway.

_____

2. Cars move in and out of the lanes.

_____

3. Trucks go past small cars.

_____

Lesson 21

Nouns

> ■ A **noun** is a word that names a person, place, thing, or quality.
> EXAMPLES: boy, Maria, river, Wyoming, house, beach, joy

A. Write nouns that name the following:

1. Four famous people

   _____   _____

   _____   _____

2. Four types of jobs

   _____   _____

   _____   _____

3. Four places you would like to visit

   _____   _____

   _____   _____

4. Four vegetables

   _____   _____

   _____   _____

5. Four qualities you would like to possess

   _____   _____

   _____   _____

B. Underline each noun.

1. Alaska is rich in gold, silver, copper, and oil.

2. Chocolate is made from the beans of a tree that grows in the tropics.

3. The distance across Texas is greater than the distance from Chicago to New York.

4. The men and women rode their horses in the parade.

5. The oldest city in California is San Diego.

6. Alexander Graham Bell, the inventor of the telephone, was born in Edinburgh, Scotland.

7. Jack, Diane, and I took a plane to London, where we saw Buckingham Palace.

8. Many interesting animals, such as piranhas, alligators, anacondas, and sloths,

   live in the Amazon River Basin.

9. The tarantula is a type of large, hairy spider.

10. The Maya were a people who lived in what is now Mexico and Central America.

Lesson 22

Common and Proper Nouns

> - There are two main types of nouns: **common nouns** and **proper nouns**.
> - A **common noun** names any one of a class of objects.
>   EXAMPLES: girl, state, author
> - A **proper noun** is the name of a particular person, place, or thing. A proper noun begins with a capital letter.
>   EXAMPLES: Mark Twain, Tennessee, Washington Monument

A. Write a proper noun suggested by each common noun.

1. college _____

2. river _____

3. governor _____

4. singer _____

5. physician _____

6. holiday _____

7. TV show _____

8. city _____

9. teacher _____

10. classmate _____

11. car _____

12. school _____

13. lake _____

14. country _____

15. street _____

16. park _____

17. month _____

18. actor _____

19. girl _____

20. state _____

B. Write a common noun suggested by each proper noun.

1. Alaska _____

2. South America _____

3. Tuesday _____

4. Nile _____

5. Dr. Washington _____

6. Lake Superior _____

7. Thanksgiving _____

8. Pacific _____

9. Arizona _____

10. David _____

11. Mars _____

12. Bill Clinton _____

13. February _____

14. Andes Mountains _____

15. Mexico _____

16. *Treasure Island* _____

17. Jennifer _____

18. Paris _____

19. Washington, D.C. _____

20. Fido _____

C. Underline each common noun.

1. The sturdy <u>timber</u> of the <u>oak</u> is used in constructing <u>furniture</u>, <u>bridges</u>, and <u>ships</u>.
2. Robert Fulton was a painter, jeweler, farmer, engineer, and inventor.
3. The main crops of Puerto Rico are sugar, tobacco, coffee, and fruits.
4. The pecan groves of Texas provide nuts for the eastern part of the United States.
5. France has many rivers and beaches.
6. The Verrazano-Narrows Bridge between Brooklyn and Staten Island is the longest suspension bridge in the world.
7. Some of the main foods eaten in Greece are lamb, fish, olives, and feta cheese.
8. A road passes through a tunnel cut in the base of a giant tree in California.
9. Since the earliest civilizations, gold has been used for ornaments.
10. One of the largest lakes in North America is Lake Erie.
11. The orange tree bears beautiful blossoms and delicious fruits.
12. Rockefeller Center is a large business and entertainment center in New York.
13. Pine trees give us turpentine, tar, resin, timber, and oils.
14. The United States buys the greatest amount of the world's coffee.
15. The pelican, the penguin, and the flamingo are interesting birds.
16. The first trip into space was filled with danger.

D. Underline each proper noun.

1. The principal goods exported by Brazil are soybeans, sugar, and coffee.
2. William Penn was the founder of Pennsylvania.
3. On the shelves of the Elm Grove Library, you will find many magical stories.
4. Commander Byrd, a naval officer, made the first airplane flight to the North Pole.
5. Dr. Jeanne Spurlock went to Howard University College of Medicine.
6. The orange tree was brought to Europe from Asia.
7. Colombia is the world's leading producer of emeralds.
8. Kilimanjaro is the tallest mountain in Africa.
9. The Navajo make beautiful silver and turquoise jewelry.
10. Leticia and Carlos anchored the tent while Sam and Ted prepared the food.
11. Thomas Jefferson introduced the decimal system of coinage (dollars, dimes, cents) that is now used in the United States.
12. Their home is on the shore of Lake Michigan.
13. Quebec is the only city in North America that has a wall around it.
14. Paul Revere was a patriot, a silversmith, an engraver, and a dentist.
15. Lemons were first grown in the valleys of India.
16. The Sears Tower in Chicago is the tallest building in the world.

Singular and Plural Nouns

- A **singular noun** names one person, place, or thing.
  EXAMPLES: girl, half, pear, sky
- A **plural noun** names more than one person, place, or thing.
  EXAMPLES: girls, halves, pears, skies
- Add -s to most nouns to make them plural.
  EXAMPLES: girl, girls   top, tops
- Add -es to most nouns ending in -ch, -sh, -s, or -x to make them plural.
  EXAMPLES: church, churches   brush, brushes   ax, axes
- If a noun ends in a consonant and -y, change the -y to -i and add -es.
  EXAMPLES: city, cities   army, armies
- If a noun ends in a vowel and -y, add -s to make it plural.
  EXAMPLE: boy, boys

A. Write the plural form for each noun below.

1. newspaper _____

2. guess _____

3. town _____

4. valley _____

5. body _____

6. story _____

7. bush _____

8. office _____

9. tax _____

10. toy _____

11. boss _____

12. school _____

13. day _____

14. copy _____

15. author _____

16. porch _____

B. Complete each sentence with the plural form of the noun in parentheses.

1. (penny)   How many _____ make a dollar?

2. (dress)   Marcy makes all of her own_____.

3. (bridge)   How many _____ were destroyed by the flood?

4. (brush)   Mr. Perez got two new _____ yesterday.

5. (county)   How many _____ are there in your state?

6. (fox)   Seven _____ live at the zoo.

7. (book)   I like to read _____ about our pioneers.

8. (lunch)   She made several _____ before school.

9. (country)   How many _____ are there in South America?

- Some nouns ending in -f or -fe are made plural by changing the -f or -fe to -ves.
  - EXAMPLES: loaf, loaves   wife, wives
- Some nouns ending in -f are made plural by adding -s.
  - EXAMPLES: roof, roofs   bluff, bluffs
- Most nouns ending in -o that have a vowel just before the -o are made plural by adding -s.
  - EXAMPLE: radio, radios
- Some nouns ending in -o preceded by a consonant are made plural by adding -es, but others are made plural by adding only -s.
  - EXAMPLES: potato, potatoes   piano, pianos
- A few nouns have irregular plural forms.
  - EXAMPLES: child, children   man, men   ox, oxen
- A few nouns have the same form for both the singular and plural.
  - EXAMPLES: trout, trout   sheep, sheep

C. Write the plural form for each noun below. You might wish to check the spellings in a dictionary.

1. knife _____

2. loaf _____

3. half _____

4. mouse _____

5. foot _____

6. goose _____

7. hoof _____

8. moose _____

9. life _____

10. tomato _____

11. tooth _____

12. piano _____

D. Complete each sentence with the plural form of the word in parentheses. You may wish to check the spellings in a dictionary.

1. (foot)   My new shoes pinch my _____.

2. (sheep)   The shepherd always takes good care of the _____.

3. (chimney)   Many _____ were blown down during the recent storm.

4. (city)   Many _____ are establishing recreation centers.

5. (leaf)   The high winds scattered the dead _____ over the yard.

6. (Mosquito)   _____ breed wherever there is standing water.

7. (nickel)   I have five Jefferson _____.

8. (friend)   Her _____ arrived on the bus yesterday.

9. (desk)   New _____ have been ordered for our office.

10. (bench)   Concrete _____ have been placed along the walk.

Lesson
24

Possessive Nouns

- A **possessive noun** shows possession of the noun that follows.
- Form the possessive of most singular nouns by adding an apostrophe (') and -s.
  - EXAMPLES: the boy's hat   Mr. Thomas's car
- Form the possessive of a plural noun ending in -s by adding only an apostrophe.
  - EXAMPLES: the Smiths' home   girls' bikes   sisters' names
- Form the possessive of a plural noun that does not end in -s by adding an apostrophe and -s.
  - EXAMPLES: children's classes   men's books

A. Write the possessive form of each noun.

1. girl _____girl's_____
2. child _____
3. women _____
4. children _____
5. John _____

6. baby _____
7. boys _____
8. teacher _____
9. Dr. Ray _____
10. ladies _____

11. brother _____
12. soldier _____
13. men _____
14. aunt _____
15. Ms. Jones _____

B. Rewrite each phrase using a possessive noun.

1. the cap belonging to Jim _____Jim's cap_____
2. the wrench that belongs to Kathy _____
3. the smile of the baby _____
4. the car that my friend owns _____
5. the new shoes that belong to Kim _____
6. the collar of the dog _____
7. the golf clubs that Frank owns _____
8. the shoes that belong to the runners _____
9. the friends of our parents _____
10. the opinion of the editor _____
11. the lunches of the children _____
12. the coat belonging to Kyle _____
13. the assignment of the teacher _____

Lesson 28

Helping Verbs

> ■ The last word of a verb phrase is the main verb. The other words are **helping verbs.**
>
> helping verb   main verb
>
> EXAMPLES: Beth and Jon **were** **sitting** on the bench.
> Apples **are** **displayed** by the produce manager.
>
> ■ The helping verbs are:
> am, are, is, was, were, be, being, been
> has, have, had
> do, does, did
> can, could, must, may, might, shall, should, will, would

A. Underline the verb phrase, and circle the helping verb in each sentence below.

1. We (have) begun our spring cleaning.

2. Molly and Anne will rake the leaves on the front lawn.

3. Vincent and April must sweep the driveway.

4. The twins, Dawn and Daniela, will pull the weeds.

5. Christopher and his cousin, Lisa, may prepare lunch for the workers.

6. They should wash their hands first.

7. Sandwiches and fruit salad would make a delicious lunch on a hot day.

8. Our next-door neighbor is working on his lawn, too.

9. He has sprayed his front and back lawns with a fertilizer.

10. Every helper must close the garbage bags tightly.

11. Squirrels, raccoons, and large crows would enjoy our garbage.

12. We might finish the outside work today.

B. Use each verb phrase in a sentence.

1. would come _____

2. should choose _____

3. had bought _____

4. might find _____

5. am writing _____

6. will learn _____

7. could become _____

8. were standing _____

More Helping Verbs

> ■ A verb phrase may have more than one helping verb.
>
> helping verb   main verb
> ↓   ↓
> EXAMPLES: Bill **should have   taken** the bus.
> My tomato plants **have been   growing** very quickly.
>
> ■ In a question or a sentence containing a word such as <u>not</u> or <u>never</u>, the helping verb might be separated from the main verb.
> EXAMPLES: When **will** you **decide** to fix your bicycle?
> Jason **has** not **fixed** his bicycle.

A. Underline the verb phrases, and circle the helping verbs in the sentences below.

1. Our final exam will be given on May 10.

2. Many students have been studying every night.

3. My friends and I may be forming a study group.

4. The study group members should be reviewing each chapter.

5. Are you joining our study group?

6. May we meet in your house one afternoon next week?

7. Kim and Tim should have known the answers to the first ten questions.

8. Where have you been all day?

9. I have been looking everywhere for you.

10. I would have met you earlier.

11. The airplane flight has been delayed in Chicago.

12. Would you prefer an earlier flight?

13. No, I had been enjoying a long visit with my grandmother.

14. My parents have been waiting for over two hours in the airport.

15. Lois and Jeanine had been at the pool all day.

16. Will any other friends be swimming in the pool?

17. Several neighborhood children must have been splashing each other.

18. Could Jessica and I take diving lessons next summer?

B. Use each verb phrase in a statement.

1. should have bought _____

2. had been finished _____

C. Use each verb phrase in a question.

1. will be going _____

2. have been practicing _____

Using *Is/Are* and *Was/Were*

- Use <u>is</u> with a singular subject.
  - EXAMPLE: Tasha **is** the winner.
- Use <u>are</u> with a plural subject.
  - EXAMPLE: The boys **are** walking home.
- Always use <u>are</u> with the pronoun <u>you</u>.
  - EXAMPLE: <u>You</u> **are** absolutely right!

A. Underline the correct verb to complete each sentence.

1. (Is, Are) this tool ready to be cleaned?

2. They (is, are) making peanut brittle.

3. Bill (is, are) the chairperson this week.

4. Where (is, are) my gloves?

5. This tomato (is, are) too ripe.

6. Ryan, (is, are) these your books?

7. Daniel, (is, are) the sandwiches ready?

8. (Is, Are) you going to sing your solo this morning?

9. This newspaper (is, are) the early edition.

10. Carol asked if you (is, are) still coming to the game.

- Use <u>was</u> with a singular subject to tell about the past.
  - EXAMPLE: I **was** there yesterday.
- Use <u>were</u> with a plural subject to tell about the past.
  - EXAMPLE: Kevin and Ray **were** not home.
- Always use <u>were</u> with the pronoun <u>you</u>.
  - EXAMPLE: <u>You</u> **were** only a few minutes late.

B. Underline the correct verb to complete each sentence.

1. Amy and Crystal (was, were) disappointed because they could not go.

2. Our seats (was, were) near the stage.

3. Taro, Bill, and Luis (was, were) assigned to the first team.

4. These pencils (was, were) made by a company in Chicago.

5. There (was, were) only one carton of milk in the refrigerator.

6. Who (was, were) that person on the corner?

7. She (was, were) at my house this morning.

8. You (was, were) the best swimmer in the contest.

9. Those tomatoes (was, were) delicious!

10. He (was, were) late for work today.

- The **tense** of a verb tells the time of the action or being.
- **Present tense** tells that something is happening now.
    EXAMPLES: Amanda **dances** in the show. My art lessons **start** today.
- **Past tense** tells that something happened in the past. The action is over.
    EXAMPLES: Amanda **danced** in the show.
    My art lessons **started** last June.
- **Future tense** tells that something will happen in the future. Use will with the verb.
    EXAMPLES: Amanda **will dance** in the show.
    My art lessons **will start** next month.

A. Underline the verb or verb phrase in each sentence. Then write present, past, or future for the tense of each verb.

1. My neighbor works four days a week. _____

2. Sometimes I care for her children, Karen and Billy. _____

3. They play in front of my house. _____

4. One day Karen threw the ball very hard to Billy. _____

5. The ball sailed over Billy's head and into the street. _____

6. Billy ran toward the street. _____

7. I shouted to Billy. _____

8. Usually, Billy listens to me. _____

9. I got the ball from the street. _____

10. Billy's mom called for him to come home. _____

11. He went as fast as possible. _____

12. Next time they will play only in the backyard. _____

B. Rewrite each sentence, changing the underlined verb to the past tense.

1. My little sister will follow me everywhere.

_____

2. She comes to my friend's house.

_____

3. She rides my bicycle on the grass.

_____

Lesson 32

Principal Parts of Verbs

- A verb has four principal parts: **present, present participle, past,** and **past participle.**
- For **regular verbs,** the present participle is formed by adding -ing to the present. It is used with a form of the helping verb be.
- The past and past participles are formed by adding -ed to the present. The past participle uses a form of the helping verb have.

  EXAMPLES:

Present	Present Participle	Past	Past Participle
walk	(is) walking	walked	(have, has, had) walked
point	(is) pointing	pointed	(have, has, had) pointed
cook	(is) cooking	cooked	(have, has, had) cooked

- **Irregular verbs** form their past and past participles in other ways. A dictionary shows the principal parts of these verbs.

- Write the present participle, past, and past participle for each verb.

PRESENT	PRESENT PARTICIPLE	PAST	PAST PARTICIPLE
1. walk	(is) walking	walked	(have, has, had) walked
2. visit			
3. watch			
4. follow			
5. jump			
6. talk			
7. add			
8. learn			
9. paint			
10. plant			
11. work			
12. divide			
13. miss			
14. score			
15. call			
16. collect			

Unit 3, Grammar and Usage

- Never use a helping verb with: <u>saw</u>   <u>did</u>   <u>came</u>
- Always use a helping verb with: <u>seen</u>   <u>done</u>   <u>come</u>

■ **Underline the correct verb form to complete each sentence.**

1. We (saw, seen) the movie.

2. Suddenly, the whole idea (came, come) to me.

3. Tammy and John (did, done) not do the ironing this morning.

4. They (saw, seen) that a lot of work had to be done to the camp.

5. Who (did, done) the framing of these prints?

6. The rain (came, come) down in sheets.

7. I haven't (did, done) all the errands for Anna.

8. I have (came, come) to help arrange the stage.

9. We have (saw, seen) many miles of beautiful prairie flowers.

10. What have you (did, done) with the kittens?

11. My uncle (came, come) to help me move.

12. I have not (saw, seen) the new apartment today.

13. Why haven't your brothers (came, come) to help us?

14. Haven't you ever (saw, seen) a spider spinning a web?

15. When Lynne and I (came, come) in, we found a surprise.

16. I (saw, seen) the owner about the job.

17. We saw what you (did, done)!

18. Has the mail (came, come) yet?

19. The prettiest place we (saw, seen) was the Grand Canyon.

20. Hasn't Kyle (did, done) a nice job of painting the room?

21. Mr. Jones (came, come) to repair the stove.

22. My dog, Max, (did, done) that trick twice.

23. Josh hadn't (came, come) to the soccer game.

24. Rebecca (saw, seen) the doctor yesterday.

25. Scott has (came, come) to the picnic.

26. Who has (saw, seen) the Rocky Mountains?

27. Deb (did, done) the decorations for the party.

28. She (came, come) to the party an hour early.

29. The bird (saw, seen) the cat near the tree.

30. The painter has (did, done) a nice job on the house.

■ Never use a helping verb with: ate   drank
■ Always use a helping verb with: <u>eaten</u>   <u>drunk</u>

A. Underline the correct verb form to complete each sentence.

1. Have the worms (ate, eaten) the leaves on that tree?

2. We (drank, drunk) the spring water from the mountains.

3. You (ate, eaten) more for breakfast than I did.

4. Haven't you (drank, drunk) a glass of this refreshing lemonade?

5. The hungry hikers (ate, eaten) quickly.

6. Yes, I (drank, drunk) two glasses of lemonade.

7. Have you (ate, eaten) your lunch so soon?

8. Maggie, why haven't you (drank, drunk) your tea?

9. I (ate, eaten) two delicious hamburgers for lunch.

10. We watched the birds as they (drank, drunk) from the birdbath.

11. We (ate, eaten) supper early.

12. Who (drank, drunk) a glass of tomato juice?

13. Have you ever (ate, eaten) a pink grapefruit?

14. Elizabeth, have you (drank, drunk) an extra glass of milk?

15. Have you (ate, eaten) your breakfast yet?

16. Yes, I (drank, drunk) it about noon.

B. Write the correct past tense form of each verb in parentheses to complete each sentence.

1. (eat)   Maria had _____ turkey and stuffing at Thanksgiving.

2. (drink)   She _____ cranberry juice for breakfast.

3. (eat)   Carlos _____ a second sandwich.

4. (drink)   At the picnic we had _____ a gallon of lemonade.

5. (drink)   Yes, I _____ it at about noon.

6. (eat)   Cory hasn't _____ since breakfast.

7. (drink)   Father _____ a glass of iced tea.

8. (eat)   Did you know that those apples had been _____?

9. (drink)   Haven't Mike and Lisa _____ the fresh orange juice?

10. (eat)   The people on the train _____ in the dining car.

Past Tenses of *Sing* and *Ring*

- Never use a helping verb with: <u>sang</u> <u>rang</u>
- Always use a helping verb with: <u>sung</u> <u>rung</u>

A. Underline the correct verb form to complete each sentence.

1. I have never (sang, sung) in public before.

2. Have the church bells (rang, rung)?

3. The group (sang, sung) all their college songs for us.

4. The bell had not (rang, rung) at five o'clock.

5. The children (sang, sung) three patriotic songs.

6. We (rang, rung) their doorbell several times.

7. Which of the three sisters (sang, sung) in the talent show?

8. Who (rang, rung) the outside bell?

9. Patti, have you ever (sang, sung) for the choir director?

10. I (rang, rung) the large old bell that is beside the door.

11. Has she ever (sang, sung) this duet?

12. The Liberty Bell hasn't (rang, rung) in many years.

13. The group (sang, sung) as they had never (sang, sung) before.

14. The ship's bell hasn't (rang, rung).

15. The Canadian singer often (sang, sung) that song.

16. Have you (rang, rung) the bell on that post?

B. Write the correct past tense form of the verb in parentheses to complete each sentence.

1. (ring)   It was so noisy that we couldn't tell if the bell had _____.

2. (sing)   Maria _____ a solo.

3. (sing)   She had never _____ alone before.

4. (ring)   The bells _____ to announce their marriage yesterday.

5. (ring)   Have you _____ the bell yet?

6. (sing)   Who _____ the first song?

7. (ring)   The group _____ bells to play a tune.

8. (sing)   Hasn't she _____ before royalty?

9. (ring)   The boxer jumped up as the bell _____.

10. (sing)   That young boy _____ a solo.

Past Tenses of *Freeze, Choose, Speak,* and *Break*

- Never use a helping verb with: <u>froze</u> <u>chose</u> <u>spoke</u> <u>broke</u>
- Always use a helping verb with: <u>frozen</u> <u>chosen</u> <u>spoken</u> <u>broken</u>

A. Underline the correct verb form to complete each sentence.

1. Haven't those candidates (spoke, spoken) yet?

2. Has the dessert (froze, frozen) in the molds?

3. I (broke, broken) the handle of the hammer.

4. Have you (spoke, spoken) to your friends about the meeting?

5. Hadn't the coach (chose, chosen) the best players today?

6. The dog has (broke, broken) the toy.

7. Has Anna (spoke, spoken) to you about going with us?

8. We (froze, frozen) the ice for our picnic.

9. I believe you (chose, chosen) the right clothes.

10. Dave, haven't you (broke, broken) your bat?

11. Mr. Mann (spoke, spoken) first.

12. Anthony (froze, frozen) the fruit salad for our picnic.

13. You didn't tell me he had (broke, broken) his arm.

14. The men on the team (chose, chosen) their plays carefully.

15. Ms. Ramirez (spoke, spoken) first.

16. Has the river (froze, frozen) yet?

B. Write the correct past tense form of the verb in parentheses to complete each sentence.

1. (freeze)   We could not tell if the ice had _____ overnight.

2. (break)   The chain on Ann's bicycle had _____ while she rode.

3. (choose)   Carol had _____ to be in the play.

4. (speak)   No one _____ while the band played.

5. (choose)   Tom has _____ to take both tests today.

6. (choose)   Jim _____ not to take the test early.

7. (break)   No one knew who had _____ the window.

8. (speak)   Carol _____ her lines loudly and clearly.

9. (freeze)   It was so cold that everything had _____.

10. (speak)   The librarian wanted to know who had _____ so loudly.

Past Tenses of *Know, Grow,* and *Throw*

- Never use a helping verb with: <u>knew</u> <u>grew</u> <u>threw</u>
- Always use a helping verb with: <u>known</u> <u>grown</u> <u>thrown</u>

A. Underline the correct verb form to complete each sentence.

1. We have (knew, known) her family for years.

2. Weeds (grew, grown) along the park paths.

3. Hasn't Julia (threw, thrown) the softball?

4. I have never (knew, known) a more courageous person.

5. Katie's plants have (grew, grown) very rapidly.

6. How many times have you (threw, thrown) at the target?

7. Has Jonathan (grew, grown) any unusual plants this year?

8. I (knew, known) every person at the meeting.

9. I wish that my hair hadn't (grew, grown) so much this year.

10. Brian, how long have you (knew, known) Lee?

11. The pitcher has (threw, thrown) three strikes in a row.

12. I don't know why the plants (grew, grown) so fast.

13. We (threw, thrown) out many old boxes.

14. Mr. Low has (grew, grown) vegetables this summer.

15. Marty (knew, known) the correct answer.

16. The guard (threw, thrown) the ball to the center.

17. She is the nicest person I have ever (knew, known).

18. The sun (grew, grown) brighter in the afternoon.

B. Write one original sentence with <u>knew</u>. Then write one sentence with <u>known</u>.

1. _____

2. _____

C. Write one original sentence with <u>grew</u>. Then write one sentence with <u>grown</u>.

1. _____

2. _____

D. Write one original sentence with <u>threw</u>. Then write one sentence with <u>thrown</u>.

1. _____

2. _____

Past Tenses of *Blow* and *Fly*

> ■ Never use a helping verb with: <u>blew</u>   <u>flew</u>
> ■ Always use a helping verb with: <u>blown</u>   <u>flown</u>

A. Underline the correct verb form to complete each sentence.

1. Flags (flew, flown) from many houses on the Fourth of July.

2. The train whistles have (blew, blown) at every crossing.

3. The birds haven't (flew, flown) south for the winter.

4. The wind (blew, blown) the kites to pieces.

5. The candles (blew, blown) out too soon.

6. Has your friend (flew, flown) her new kite?

7. Yes, she (flew, flown) it this morning.

8. All the papers have (blew, blown) across the floor.

9. Four people (flew, flown) their model airplanes in the tournament.

10. The wind has (blew, blown) like this for an hour.

11. I didn't know that you had (flew, flown) here in a jet.

12. Hasn't the train whistle (blew, blown) yet?

13. The airplanes (flew, flown) in an aviation show.

14. Our largest maple tree had (blew, blown) down last night.

15. The striped hot-air balloon has (flew, flown) the farthest.

16. The judge (blew, blown) the whistle as the runner crossed the finish line.

17. The Carsons have (flew, flown) to Europe.

18. An erupting volcano (blew, blown) the mountain apart.

19. The geese (flew, flown) in formation.

20. The curtains have (blew, blown) open from the breeze.

21. The movie star (flew, flown) in a private jet.

22. A tornado (blew, blown) the roof off a house.

23. A pair of ducks has (flew, flown) overhead.

B. Write one original sentence with <u>blew</u>. Then write one sentence with <u>blown</u>.

1. _____

2. _____

C. Write one original sentence with <u>flew</u>. Then write one sentence with <u>flown</u>.

1. _____

2. _____

Past Tenses of *Take* and *Write*

> ■ Never use a helping verb with: <u>took</u>   <u>wrote</u>
> ■ Always use a helping verb with: <u>taken</u>   <u>written</u>

A. Underline the correct verb form to complete each sentence.

1. They (took, taken) the first plane to Tampa.

2. Who has (wrote, written) the best script for the play?

3. Mike hadn't (took, taken) these pictures last summer.

4. Who (wrote, written) the minutes of our last meeting?

5. We (took, taken) down our paintings.

6. Marguerite Henry has (wrote, written) many stories about horses.

7. I (took, taken) my watch to the jeweler for repair.

8. I (wrote, written) for a video catalog.

9. Haven't you (took, taken) your medicine yet?

10. Diana, have you (wrote, written) to your friend?

11. Carlos (took, taken) too much time getting ready.

12. Diane hadn't (wrote, written) these exercises with a pen.

13. Who (took, taken) my magazine?

14. Mario (wrote, written) an excellent business letter.

B. Write the correct past tense form of the verb in parentheses to complete each sentence.

1. (write)   Who _____ this short theme?

2. (take)   It has _____ me a long time to make this planter.

3. (write)   Eve Merriam had _____ this poem.

4. (take)   The children have _____ off their muddy shoes.

5. (write)   We _____ letters to our state senators.

6. (take)   Louisa, have you _____ your dog for a walk?

7. (write)   My cousin _____ me a letter about his new house.

8. (write)   Robert Frost _____ David's favorite poem.

9. (take)   Willie and Sharon _____ the bus to the park.

10. (write)   Mr. Bustos _____ an excellent article for our newspaper.

11. (take)   The nurse _____ my temperature.

Past Tenses of *Give* and *Go*

> ■ Never use a helping verb with: <u>gave</u>   <u>went</u>
> ■ Always use a helping verb with: <u>given</u>   <u>gone</u>

A. **Underline the correct verb form to complete each sentence.**

1. Ms. Morris has (gave, given) that land to the city.

2. Where has Ann (went, gone) this afternoon?

3. Carlos (gave, given) a speech on collecting rare coins.

4. My friends (went, gone) to the park an hour ago.

5. Mary, who (gave, given) you this ruby ring?

6. Rob and Carter have (went, gone) to paint the house.

7. Mr. Edwards (gave, given) us ten minutes to take the test.

8. Elaine has (went, gone) to help Eileen find the place.

9. My friends (gave, given) clothing to the people whose house burned.

10. Hasn't Jan (went, gone) to the store yet?

11. The sportscaster has just (gave, given) the latest baseball scores.

12. Charlie (went, gone) to apply for the job.

13. Have you (gave, given) Fluffy her food?

14. Has Miss Martinson (went, gone) to Springfield?

15. I have (gave, given) my horn to my cousin.

16. Paula has (went, gone) to sleep already.

B. **Write the correct past tense form of the verb in parentheses to complete each sentence.**

1. (go)   Paula _____ to sleep already.

2. (give)   Has Mrs. Tate _____ the checks to the other employees?

3. (go)   Every person had _____ before you arrived.

4. (give)   My neighbor was _____ a ticket for speeding.

5. (go)   Haven't the Yamadas _____ to Japan for a month?

6. (give)   Ms. O'Malley has _____ me a notebook.

7. (go)   Haven't you ever _____ to an aquarium?

8. (give)   I _____ her my new address.

9. (go)   Michael _____ to camp for a week.

10. (give)   Ms. Rosen has _____ me driving lessons.

Possessive Pronouns

- A **possessive pronoun** is a pronoun that shows ownership of something.
- The possessive pronouns <u>hers</u>, <u>mine</u>, <u>ours</u>, <u>theirs</u>, and <u>yours</u> stand alone.
  EXAMPLES: The coat is **mine.** The shoes are **yours.**
- The possessive pronouns <u>her</u>, <u>its</u>, <u>my</u>, <u>our</u>, <u>their</u>, and <u>your</u> must be used before nouns.
  EXAMPLES: **Her** car is red. **Our** car is black.
- The pronoun <u>his</u> may be used either way.
  EXAMPLES: That is **his** dog. The dog is **his.**

■ **Underline the possessive pronoun in each sentence.**

1. Lora lost her bracelet.

2. David broke his arm.

3. The dogs wagged their tails.

4. The referee blew her whistle.

5. The students should take their books.

6. Musician Louis Armstrong was famous for his smile.

7. Brad entered his sculpture in the contest.

8. I wanted to read that book, but a number of its pages are missing.

9. My aunt and uncle have sold their Arizona ranch.

10. The Inuit build their igloos out of snow blocks.

11. How did Florida get its name?

12. David showed the group his wonderful stamp collection.

13. Coffee found its way from Arabia to Java.

14. The magpie builds its nest very carefully.

15. Pam sprained her ankle while skiing.

16. Lisa drove her car to the top of the peak.

17. Frank left his raincoat in the doctor's office.

18. Isn't Alaska noted for its salmon?

19. Travis brought his mother a beautiful shawl from India.

20. Gina, where is your brother?

21. Manuel forgot about his appointment with the dentist.

22. Joel and Andrew have gone to their swimming lesson.

23. Sandra showed her report to the boss.

24. Juan gave his father a beautiful paperweight.

25. Mr. Owens found his keys.

26. The children broke their swing.

Indefinite Pronouns

- An **indefinite pronoun** is a pronoun that does not refer to a specific person or thing.
  - EXAMPLES: **Someone** is coming to speak to the group.
  - Does **anyone** know what time it is?
  - **Everybody** is looking forward to the trip.
- Some indefinite pronouns are negative.
  - EXAMPLES: **Nobody** has a ticket.
  - **No one** was waiting at the bus stop.
- The indefinite pronouns <u>anybody</u>, <u>anyone</u>, <u>anything</u>, <u>each</u>, <u>everyone</u>, <u>everybody</u>, <u>everything</u>, <u>nobody</u>, <u>no one</u>, <u>nothing</u>, <u>somebody</u>, <u>someone</u>, and <u>something</u> are singular. They take singular verbs.
  - EXAMPLE: **Everyone is** ready.
- The indefinite pronouns <u>both</u>, <u>few</u>, <u>many</u>, <u>several</u>, and <u>some</u> are plural. They take plural verbs.
  - EXAMPLE: **Several** of us **are** ready.

A. Underline the indefinite pronoun in each sentence below.

1. Everyone helped complete the project.

2. Is somebody waiting for you?

3. Anything is possible.

4. Something arrived in the mail.

5. Everybody looked tired at practice.

6. No one was willing to work longer.

7. Does anyone have a dollar?

8. Both of us were tired.

9. Nothing was dry yet.

10. Does anybody want to go swimming?

11. Someone should speak up.

12. Everybody is hungry now.

13. Each of the cats was black.

14. Some of the dogs bark all the time.

15. Several were empty.

16. No one remembered to bring it.

17. Everyone started to feel nervous.

18. Nobody admitted to being afraid.

19. Everything will be explained.

20. Is anything missing?

B. Complete each sentence with an indefinite pronoun.

1. I can't believe that _____ in my desk has disappeared.

2. Is _____ coming to teach you to run the computer?

3. Every person in class attended today. _____ was absent.

4. She tried to call, but _____ answered the phone.

5. Does _____ remember the address?

6. There is _____ here to see you.

7. Would _____ like a piece of cake?

8. The party was so much fun. _____ enjoyed it.

Lesson 43

Subject Pronouns

> - A **subject pronoun** is used as the subject or as part of the subject of a sentence.
> - The subject pronouns are I, you, he, she, it, we, and they.
>   EXAMPLE: **It** has beautiful wings.
> - When the pronoun I is used with nouns or other pronouns, it is always named last.
>   EXAMPLE: Marie and **I** caught a butterfly.

■ **Underline the correct pronoun.**

1. Carolyn and (I, me) helped repair the car.

2. (She, Her) is going to the studio.

3. Why can't Leigh and (I, me) go with them?

4. (She, Her) and Charles skated all afternoon.

5. Jaclyn and (I, me) are going to Chicago tomorrow.

6. (He, Him) played tennis this morning.

7. Beth and (he, him) were five minutes late yesterday morning.

8. (She, Her) and (I, me) spent an hour in the library.

9. Joanne and (I, me) worked until nine o'clock.

10. (He, Him) and Yuri are going over there now.

11. May (we, us) carry your packages?

12. (They, Them) and I are buying some groceries.

13. Sarah and (I, me) are going with her to the park.

14. (It, Them) wagged its tail.

15. (She, You) have a beautiful singing voice, Claire.

16. (He, Him) is the owner of the suitcase.

17. Crystal and (I, me) are on the same team.

18. (She, Her) has started a book club.

19. (We, Us) are planning a bike trip.

20. (They, Them) are going to see a Shakespearean play.

21. Is (she, her) your favorite singer?

22. Martin and (I, me) would be happy to help you.

23. (We, Us) work at the post office.

24. Juan and (we, us) are painting the front porch.

25. (He, Him) excels as a photographer.

26. (She, Her) has known us for several years.

27. (I, Me) am the director of the community choir.

- An **object pronoun** is used after an action verb or a preposition, such as <u>after</u>, <u>against</u>, <u>at</u>, <u>between</u>, <u>except</u>, <u>for</u>, <u>from</u>, <u>in</u>, <u>of</u>, <u>to</u>, and <u>with</u>.
- The object pronouns are <u>me</u>, <u>you</u>, <u>him</u>, <u>her</u>, <u>it</u>, <u>us</u>, and <u>them</u>.
  EXAMPLE: The gift was for **him.**
- When the pronoun <u>me</u> is used with nouns or other pronouns, it is always last.
  EXAMPLE: The books were for Kay and **me.**

- **Underline the correct pronoun.**

1. Tony, are you going with Stephanie and (I, me) to see Rosa?

2. Scott invited Patrick and (I, me) to a movie.

3. I am going to see Mary and (she, her) about this problem.

4. The woman told (us, we) to come for her old magazines.

5. I went with Jan and (she, her) to the hobby show.

6. That dinner was prepared by (them, they).

7. James asked Andrew and (I, me) to the soccer game.

8. Emily and Bev congratulated (he, him).

9. Sharon praised (him, he) for his work.

10. Will you talk to (she, her) about the trip?

11. Ben, can you go with Renee and (I, me)?

12. Pam lectured (us, we) about being on time.

13. The package was leaning against (it, we).

14. They brought the problem to (we, us).

15. It was too hard for (they, them) to solve.

16. Richard gave (I, me) his old goalie's equipment.

17. Anthony is teaching (we, us) Morse code.

18. Please inform (he, him) of the change of plans.

19. Brian offered to help (I, me) hang the curtains.

20. That car belongs to (he, him).

21. Carl didn't see (they, them).

22. Nancy asked him to take a picture of (we, us).

23. Please wait for (she, her) after school.

24. She is in the class with (he, him).

25. Hand the packages to (they, them).

26. Was this really discovered by (she, her)?

27. Would you like to go to dinner with (we, us)?

Subject Pronouns After Linking Verbs

■ A **linking verb** connects the subject of a sentence with a noun or adjective that comes after the linking verb.

                       Subject   Linking Verb   Noun

EXAMPLES: The **baby**   was   **Christopher.**

           The **baseball players**   were   **my friends.**

■ Use a subject pronoun after a linking verb.

EXAMPLES: The **baby**   was   **he.**

           The **baseball players**   were   **they.**

■ Use a subject pronoun after such phrases as <u>it is</u> or <u>it was</u>.

EXAMPLE: It was **I** who asked the question.

A. Underline the correct pronoun.

1. It was (I, me) who found the keys.

2. It was (she, her) who lost them.

3. The detectives were (we, us).

4. It was (they, them) who looked in the mailbox.

5. The letter carrier is (she, her).

6. It was (he, him) on the telephone.

7. The speakers were Jerald and (I, me).

8. The athlete was (she, her).

9. The photographer was (he, him).

10. That young woman is (she, her).

11. The helper is (he, him).

12. My partners are (they, them).

13. Was it (he, him) who told you?

14. The winner of the race is (she, her).

15. It was (we, us) who were chosen.

16. Was it (I, me) who made the error?

B. Complete these sentences by writing a subject pronoun for the word or words in parentheses.

1. It was _____ who worked out in the gym.   (the basketball team)

2. The most talented gymnast is _____. (Susan)

3. Our newest team members are _____. (Jay and Mark)

4. The coach with the whistle is _____. (Laura)

5. The spectators in the gym were _____. (my friends)

6. The one who is on the parallel bars is _____. (Bob)

7. The one who is on the balance beam is _____. (Kristin)

8. Our best vaulter is _____. (Michelle)

9. The athlete on the rings was _____. (Bill)

10. The vice president of the company is _____. (Ms. Walker)

Using *Who/Whom*

- Use <u>who</u> as a subject pronoun. EXAMPLE: **Who** came to the party?
- Use <u>whom</u> as an object pronoun. EXAMPLE: **Whom** did the nurse help?
- By rearranging the sentence <u>The nurse did help **whom?**,</u> you can see that whom follows the verb and is the object of the verb. It can also be the object of a preposition. EXAMPLE: To **whom** did you wish to speak?

■ **Complete each sentence with <u>Who</u> or <u>Whom</u>.**

1. _____Who_____ is that man?

2. _____ made the first moon landing?

3. _____ would you choose as the winner?

4. _____ is your best friend?

5. _____ gets the reward?

6. _____ will be staying with you this summer?

7. _____ did the instructor invite to speak to the class?

8. _____ did you see at the park?

9. _____ will you contact at headquarters?

10. _____ will you write about?

11. _____ is available to baby-sit for me on Saturday?

12. _____ did you drive to the store?

13. _____ would like to travel to Hawaii next summer?

14. _____ raced in the track meet?

15. _____ did they meet at the airport?

16. _____ are your three favorite authors?

17. _____ owns that new blue car?

18. _____ did you help last week?

19. _____ wrote that clever poem?

20. _____ will you ask to help you move?

21. _____ brought that salad?

■ **Underline the pronouns in each sentence below.**

1. He went with us to the picnic by the lake.

2. Did you find a magazine in the living room?

3. When are we going to meet at the concert?

4. Are we leaving today?

5. Did you see him?

6. She saw them at the party.

7. He spoke to James and me.

8. Who brought the music for you to play?

9. Kristin and I invited them to go to a movie.

10. Mary brought me these pictures she took.

11. Why can't they go with us?

12. I went with her to get the application form.

13. Louis brought you and him some French coins.

14. Between you and me, I think that last program was silly.

15. Did Dorothy explain the experiment to her and him?

16. Did she find them?

17. May I go with you?

18. He and I sat on the benches.

19. They saw me this morning.

20. Who has a library book?

21. For whom shall I ask?

22. I do not have it with me.

23. She told me about the trip to Canada.

24. They are coming to see us.

25. We haven't heard from James since he left.

26. Come with us.

27. Aren't you and I going with Alan?

28. You should plan the theme before you write it.

29. Aren't they coming for us?

30. Kelly and I gave them a new book of stamps.

31. Steve told us an interesting story about a dog.

32. Who is planning a summer vacation?

33. She and I never expected to see you here!

34. We will visit them this evening.

Lesson
48 — More Pronouns

■ **Underline the correct pronoun.**

1. It was (I, me).

2. Bill and (he, him) are on their way to catch the plane.

3. Nicole and (I, me) have always been good friends.

4. The guard showed (they, them) the entrance to the building.

5. The boss told (I, me) to clean the office.

6. Please take (I, me) to lunch.

7. I am going to wait for (she, her).

8. (Who, Whom) planted those beautiful flowers?

9. Next Saturday Zachary and (I, me) are going fishing.

10. Marie came to see (us, we).

11. To (who, whom) did you send the postcard?

12. This is a secret between you and (I, me).

13. Kevin asked Carolyn to move (us, our) table.

14. The committee asked Michael, Kip, and (I, me) to help serve.

15. Did Ellen bring (she, her)?

16. Jamie told (us, we) to get to the station on time.

17. Grant and (she, her) drove the tractors.

18. (Who, Whom) bought this magazine?

19. The boss brought Matt and Kevin (them, their) checks.

20. Martin took Armando and (I, me) to work this morning.

21. With (who, whom) did you play soccer?

22. Michelle painted (she, her) kitchen yesterday.

23. Seven of (us, we) were named to the board of directors.

24. He completed all of (his, him) math problems this morning.

25. (Us, We) are going to play basketball.

26. She called for Janice and (I, me).

27. (Who, Whom) washed the windows?

28. Joyce and (I, me) will fix the broken latch.

29. We came to see (them, they).

30. Will Pamela or (I, me) go with Jason to (him, his) ranch?

31. For (who, whom) are you looking?

32. Did you know it was (her, she)?

33. Lisa and (her, she) are painting the chairs.

34. (We, Us) are going to the museum on Saturday.

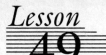

Adjectives

> ■ An **adjective** is a word that describes a noun or a pronoun.
>   EXAMPLE: The sky is spotted with **white** clouds.
> ■ Adjectives usually tell **what kind, which one,** or **how many.**
>   EXAMPLES: **white** roses, **that** mitt, **fifteen** cents

A. Choose an appropriate adjective from the box to describe each noun.

brave	foolish	gorgeous	hasty	shiny
cold	fragrant	happy	polite	sly

1. _____ scout   6. _____ girls

2. _____ flower   7. _____ sunset

3. _____ worker   8. _____ dimes

4. _____ water   9. _____ prank

5. _____ fox   10. _____ deeds

B. Write three adjectives that could be used to describe each noun.

1. flowers   _____   _____   _____

2. an automobile _____   _____   _____

3. a friend   _____   _____   _____

4. a bicycle   _____   _____   _____

5. snow   _____   _____   _____

6. a baby   _____   _____   _____

7. a sunrise   _____   _____   _____

8. a book   _____   _____   _____

9. a kitten   _____   _____   _____

10. a train   _____   _____   _____

11. a mountain   _____   _____   _____

12. the wind   _____   _____   _____

13. a river   _____   _____   _____

14. a house   _____   _____   _____

- The **articles** a, an, and the are called **limiting adjectives**.
- Use a before words beginning with a consonant sound.
  - EXAMPLES: **a** bugle, **a** mountain, **a** sail
- Use an before words beginning with a vowel sound.
  - EXAMPLES: **an** oboe, **an** island, **an** anchor

C. Write a or an in each blank.

1. _____ salesperson

2. _____ train

3. _____ newspaper

4. _____ iceberg

5. _____ friend

6. _____ election

7. _____ welder

8. _____ piano

9. _____ game

10. _____ ant

11. _____ eye

12. _____ army

13. _____ telephone

14. _____ orange

15. _____ country

16. _____ airplane

17. _____ oak

18. _____ engine

19. _____ ear

20. _____ state

21. _____ elm

22. _____ shoe

23. _____ object

24. _____ basket

25. _____ apple

26. _____ ounce

27. _____ error

28. _____ tablet

29. _____ desk

30. _____ holiday

31. _____ accident

32. _____ astronaut

33. _____ box

34. _____ fire

35. _____ pilot

36. _____ mechanic

37. _____ entrance

38. _____ evergreen

39. _____ aviator

40. _____ hundred

41. _____ picture

42. _____ elephant

43. _____ letter

44. _____ umbrella

45. _____ announcer

46. _____ onion

47. _____ umpire

48. _____ car

49. _____ ice cube

50. _____ elevator

Lesson 50

Proper Adjectives

■ A **proper adjective** is an adjective that is formed from a proper noun. It always begins with a capital letter.

EXAMPLES:	**Proper Noun**	**Proper Adjective**
	Poland	Polish
	Germany	German
	Paris	Parisian

A. Write a proper adjective formed from each proper noun below. You may wish to check the spelling in a dictionary.

1. South America _____

2. Africa _____

3. England _____

4. Mexico _____

5. France _____

6. Russia _____

7. America _____

8. Rome _____

9. Alaska _____

10. Canada _____

11. Norway _____

12. Scotland _____

13. Ireland _____

14. China _____

15. Spain _____

16. Italy _____

17. Hawaii _____

18. Japan _____

B. Write sentences using proper adjectives you formed in Exercise A.

1. _____Many South American countries have warm climates._____

2. _____

3. _____

4. _____

5. _____

6. _____

7. _____

8. _____

9. _____

10. _____

Lesson 51

Demonstrative Adjectives

- A **demonstrative adjective** is an adjective that points out a specific person or thing.
- This and that describe singular nouns. This points to a person or thing nearby, and that points to a person or thing farther away.
  - EXAMPLES: **This** room is my favorite. **That** man is running very fast.
- These and those describe plural nouns. These points to persons or things nearby, and those points to persons or things farther away.
  - EXAMPLES: **These** women are the best players. **Those** houses need painting.
- The word them is a pronoun. Never use it to describe a noun.

A. Underline the correct demonstrative adjective.

1. Please hand me (those, this) red candles.

2. Where did you buy (these, that) large pecans?

3. Did you grow (these, them) roses in your garden?

4. Please bring me (those, that) wrench.

5. Where did Marc find (these, this) watermelon?

6. (Those, Them) glasses belong to Mike.

7. Do you want one of (these, this) calendars?

8. May I use one of (these, them) pencils?

9. Did you see (those, them) films of Africa?

10. Calvin, where are (those, that) people going?

11. Did you see (those, them) police officers?

12. Please put (those, this) books in the box.

13. (That, Those) floor needs to be cleaned.

14. Sarah and Joe might buy (those, that) car.

15. (That, These) cabinets will be repainted.

16. Please close (that, those) door.

17. Will you fix the flat tire on (this, these) bike?

18. (This, Those) letter needs a stamp before you mail it.

B. Write four sentences using this, that, these, or those.

1. _____

2. _____

3. _____

4. _____

- An adjective has three degrees of comparison: **positive, comparative,** and **superlative.**
- The simple form of the adjective is called the **positive** degree.
  EXAMPLE: Anita is **tall.**
- When two people or things are being compared, the **comparative** degree is used.
  EXAMPLE: Anita is **taller** than Nancy.
- When three or more people or things are being compared, the **superlative** degree is used.
  EXAMPLE: Anita is the **tallest** person in the group.
- For all adjectives of one syllable and a few adjectives of two syllables, add -er to form the comparative degree and -est to form the superlative degree.
  EXAMPLE: rich — richer — richest
- If the adjective ends in -y, change the -y to -i and add -er or -est.
  EXAMPLE: tiny — tinier — tiniest

- **Write the comparative and superlative forms.**

POSITIVE	COMPARATIVE	SUPERLATIVE
1. smooth		
2. young		
3. sweet		
4. strong		
5. lazy		
6. great		
7. kind		
8. calm		
9. rough		
10. narrow		
11. deep		
12. short		
13. happy		
14. cold		
15. pretty		

- For some adjectives of two syllables and all adjectives of three or more syllables, use more to form the comparative and most to form the superlative.
    EXAMPLES: He thinks that the lily is **more** fragrant than the tulip.
    He thinks that the carnation is the **most** fragrant flower of all.
- Comparison of adjectives also can be used to indicate less or least of a quality. Use less to form the comparative and least to form the superlative.
    EXAMPLES: I see Jo **less** often than I see Terry.
    I see Josh **least** often of all.
- Some adjectives have irregular comparisons.
    EXAMPLES: good, better, best   bad, worse, worst

A. Write the comparative and superlative forms using <u>more</u> and <u>most</u>.

POSITIVE	COMPARATIVE	SUPERLATIVE
1. energetic		
2. courteous		
3. impatient		
4. important		
5. difficult		
6. wonderful		
7. gracious		
8. agreeable		

B. Write the comparative and superlative forms using <u>less</u> and <u>least</u>.

POSITIVE	COMPARATIVE	SUPERLATIVE
1. helpful		
2. friendly		
3. serious		
4. agreeable		
5. faithful		
6. comfortable		
7. patient		
8. reliable		

Unit 3, Grammar and Usage

C. Write the correct degree of comparison for the adjective in parentheses.

1. (near)   Which planet is _____ the earth, Venus or Jupiter?

2. (tall)   Who is the _____ of the three people?

3. (helpful)   Who is _____, Sandra or Linda?

4. (young)   Who is _____, Jack or Tim?

5. (difficult)   I think this is the _____ problem in the lesson.

6. (good)   Is "A Ghost Story" a _____ story than "The Last Leaf"?

7. (small)   What is our _____ state?

8. (hot)   In our region, August is usually the _____ month.

9. (young)   Hans is the _____ person at the factory.

10. (wide)   The Amazon is the _____ river in the world.

11. (old)   Who is _____, David or Steve?

12. (large)   What is the _____ city in your state?

13. (courteous)   Dan is always the _____ person at a party.

14. (good)   This poem is the _____ one I have read this year.

15. (cold)   This must be the _____ night so far this winter.

16. (studious)   Of the two sisters, Andrea is the _____.

17. (tall)   Who is _____, Kay or Carol?

18. (wealthy)   This is the home of the _____ banker in our city.

19. (fast)   Who is the _____ worker in the office?

20. (useful)   Which is _____, electric lights or the telephone?

21. (beautiful)   Your garden is the _____ one I have seen.

22. (narrow)   That is the _____ of all the bridges on the road.

23. (large)   Cleveland is _____ than Cincinnati.

24. (good)   Of the three books, this one is the _____.

25. (bad)   That is the _____ collection in the museum.

26. (famous)   Washington became the _____ general of the Revolution.

27. (beautiful)   I think tulips are the _____ kind of flower.

Lesson 54

Adverbs

> ■ An **adverb** is a word that describes a verb, an adjective, or another adverb.
> EXAMPLES: The parade moved **slowly.** Your tie is **very** colorful.
> You did this **too** quickly.
> ■ An adverb usually tells **how, when, where,** or **how often.**
> ■ Many adverbs end in -ly.

A. Write two adverbs that could be used to describe each verb.

1. laugh _____

_____

2. talk _____

_____

3. stand _____

_____

4. sing _____

_____

5. swim _____

_____

6. eat _____

_____

7. read _____

_____

8. work _____

_____

9. write _____

_____

10. walk _____

_____

11. jump _____

_____

12. move _____

_____

13. run _____

_____

14. speak _____

_____

15. listen _____

_____

16. drive _____

_____

17. sit _____

_____

18. dance _____

_____

B. Use each adverb in a sentence.

well	regularly	early
softly	very	here

1. _____

2. _____

3. _____

4. _____

5. _____

6. _____

C. Underline the adverb or adverbs in each sentence.

1. The old car moved slowly up the hill.

2. She answered him very quickly.

3. We arrived at the party too early, so we helped with the decorations.

4. The family waited patiently to hear about the newborn baby.

5. Cindy drove the car very cautiously in the snowstorm.

6. Does Marshall always sit here, or may I have this seat?

7. They walked very rapidly in order to get home before the rainstorm.

8. The dog ran swiftly toward its home.

9. Emily quietly waited her turn while others went ahead.

10. These oaks grow very slowly, but they are worth the long wait.

11. May I speak now, or should I wait for his call?

12. We searched everywhere for the inflatable rafts and life preservers.

13. The nights have been extremely warm, so we go swimming every evening.

14. He always speaks distinctly and practices good manners.

15. Can you swim far underwater without coming up for air?

16. Come here, and I'll show you ladybugs in the grass.

17. Please answer quickly so that we can finish before five o'clock.

18. Deer run very fast, especially at the first sign of danger.

19. I suddenly remembered that I left my jacket in the park.

20. The snow fell softly on the rooftops of the mountain village.

21. I can pack our lunches and be there by noon.

22. She wrote too rapidly and made a mistake.

23. Winters there are extremely cold, but summers are very pleasant.

24. The pianist bowed politely to the audience.

25. You are reading too rapidly to learn something from it.

26. The team played extremely well.

27. The cat walked softly toward a fly on the windowpane.

28. Everyone listened carefully to the sound of a bluebird singing.

29. We walked wearily toward the bus in the hot sun.

30. We crossed the street very carefully at the beginning of the parade.

31. We eagerly watched the game from the rooftop deck of our building.

32. The recreation center was finished recently.

33. We walked everywhere yesterday.

34. My friend dearly loves her red hat.

35. I have read this book before.

36. He wants badly to learn to play the guitar.

Comparing with Adverbs

> - An **adverb** has three degrees of comparison: **positive, comparative,** and **superlative.**
> - The simple form of the adverb is called the **positive** degree.
>   EXAMPLE: Joe worked **hard** to complete the job.
> - When two actions are being compared, the **comparative** degree is used.
>   EXAMPLE: Joe worked **harder** than Jim.
> - When three or more actions are being compared, the **superlative** degree is used.
>   EXAMPLE: Tony worked **hardest** of all.
> - Use -er to form the comparative degree and use -est to form the superlative degree of one-syllable adverbs.
> - Use more or most with longer adverbs and with adverbs that end in -ly.
>   EXAMPLE: Jan danced **more** gracefully than Tania.
>   Vicki danced the **most** gracefully of all.

■ **Complete each sentence using the comparative or superlative form of the underlined adverb.**

1. David can jump <u>high</u>. Diane can jump _____ than David.

   Donna can jump the _____ of all.

2. Grant arrives <u>late</u> for the party. Gina arrives _____

   than Grant. Gail arrives _____ of anyone.

3. Dawn walks <u>slowly</u> in the park. Tomás walks _____

   than Dawn. Sam walks _____ of all.

4. Jean spoke <u>clearly</u> before the class. Jon spoke _____

   than Jean. Joseph spoke _____ of all the students.

5. Alex scrubbed <u>hard</u>. Anne scrubbed _____ than Alex.

   Alice scrubbed the _____ of all.

6. You can lose weight <u>quickly</u> by running. A nutritious diet works _____

   than just running. Of all weight-loss programs, combining the two works

   _____.

7. Tania played the flute <u>beautifully</u>. Tara played the clarinet even _____.

   Rick played the oboe the _____ of them all.

8. Chris has been waiting <u>long</u>. Mr. Norris has been waiting even _____.

   Justin has been waiting the _____ of all.

> - Doesn't is the contraction of <u>does not</u>. Use it with singular nouns and the pronouns <u>he</u>, <u>she</u>, and <u>it</u>.
>   EXAMPLES: The dog **doesn't** want to play. She **doesn't** want to go.
> - Don't is the contraction of <u>do not</u>. Use it with plural nouns and the pronouns <u>I</u>, <u>you</u>, <u>we</u>, and <u>they</u>.
>   EXAMPLES: The children **don't** have their books. We **don't** have time.

■ **Underline the correct contraction to complete each sentence.**

1. I (doesn't, don't) know why he (doesn't, don't) like that movie star.

2. Why (doesn't, don't) the caretaker open the gates earlier?

3. (Doesn't, Don't) your sister coach the team, Tom?

4. (Doesn't, Don't) this office need more fresh air?

5. (Doesn't, Don't) this sweater belong to you, Katie?

6. We (doesn't, don't) go home at noon for lunch.

7. (Doesn't, Don't) your friend attend the state university?

8. Terry (doesn't, don't) want to miss the parade.

9. Angelo (doesn't, don't) like to play tennis.

10. It (doesn't, don't) take long to learn to swim.

11. Some of the elevators (doesn't, don't) go to the top floor.

12. Eric (doesn't, don't) know how to drive a car.

13. He (doesn't, don't) know that we are here.

14. We (doesn't, don't) listen to our radio often.

15. Why (doesn't, don't) Craig get here on time?

16. This problem (doesn't, don't) seem difficult to me.

17. (Doesn't, Don't) it look hot outside?

18. Why (doesn't, don't) Paul go, too?

19. She (doesn't, don't) want to go to the movie.

20. Kelly (doesn't, don't) have that written in her notebook.

21. (Doesn't, Don't) you want to go with us?

22. Why (doesn't, don't) your friend come to our meetings?

23. Neil (doesn't, don't) go to night school.

24. Melissa (doesn't, don't) eat ice cream.

25. Jody and Ray (doesn't, don't) like science fiction movies.

26. The people (doesn't, don't) have to wait outside.

27. (Doesn't, Don't) you want to come with us?

28. They (doesn't, don't) know if it will rain today.

> ■ Use <u>may</u> to ask for permission.
>   EXAMPLE: **May** I go with you?
> ■ Use <u>can</u> to express the ability to do something.
>   EXAMPLE: James **can** swim well.

A. Complete each sentence with <u>may</u> or <u>can</u>.

1. Adam, _____ you whistle?

2. His dog _____ do three difficult tricks.

3. Miss Nance, _____ I leave work early?

4. I _____ see the airplane in the distance.

5. Chris, _____ you tie a good knot?

6. Carlos, _____ I drive your car?

7. You _____ see the mountains from here.

8. My friend _____ drive us home.

9. The Garcias _____ speak three languages.

10. _____ I examine those new books?

> ■ <u>Teach</u> means "to give instruction."
>   EXAMPLE: I'll **teach** you how to shoot free throws.
> ■ <u>Learn</u> means "to acquire knowledge."
>   EXAMPLE: When did you **learn** to speak Spanish?

B. Complete each sentence with <u>teach</u> or <u>learn</u>.

1. I think he will _____ me quickly.

2. I will _____ to recite that poem.

3. Did Jamie _____ you to build a fire?

4. The women are going to _____ to use the new machines.

5. Will you _____ me to play tennis?

6. My brother is going to _____ Billy to skate.

7. Would you like to _____ the rules of the game to them?

8. No one can _____ you if you do not try to _____.

Using *Sit/Set* and *Lay/Lie*

- Sit means "to take a resting position." Its principal parts are sit, sitting, and sat.
  EXAMPLES: Please **sit** here. He **sat** beside her.
- Set means "to place." Its principal parts are set, setting, and set.
  EXAMPLES: Will you please **set** this dish on the table?
  She **set** the table for dinner last night.

A. Underline the correct verb.

1. Please (sit, set) down, Kathleen.

2. Where should we (sit, set) the television?

3. Where do you (sit, set)?

4. Pamela, please (sit, set) those plants out this afternoon.

5. (Sit, Set) the basket of groceries on the patio.

6. José usually (sits, sets) on this side of the table.

7. Please come and (sit, set) your books down on that desk.

8. Have you ever (sat, set) by this window?

9. Does he (sit, set) in this seat?

10. Why don't you (sit, set) over here?

- Lie means "to recline" or "to occupy a certain space." Its principal parts are lie, lying, lay, and lain.
  EXAMPLES: Why don't you **lie** down for a while?
  He **has lain** in the hammock all afternoon.
- Lay means "to place." Its principal parts are lay, laying, and laid.
  EXAMPLES: The men **are laying** new carpeting in the house.
  Who **laid** the wet towel on the table?

B. Underline the correct verb.

1. Where did you (lie, lay) your gloves, Beth?

2. (Lie, Lay) down, Spot.

3. He always (lies, lays) down to rest when he is very tired.

4. Where have you (lain, laid) the evening paper?

5. Please (lie, lay) this box on the desk.

6. Do not (lie, lay) on that dusty hay.

7. (Lay, Lie) the papers on top of the desk.

8. I (laid, lain) the shovel on that pile of dirt.

9. I need to (lie, lay) down to rest.

10. She has (laid, lain) on the sofa all morning.

Prepositions

- A **preposition** is a word that shows the relationship of a noun or a pronoun to another word in the sentence.
    EXAMPLES: Put the package **on** the table. Place the package **in** the desk.
- These are some commonly used prepositions:

about	against	at	between	from	of	through	under
above	among	behind	by	in	on	to	upon
across	around	beside	for	into	over	toward	with

- **Draw a line under each preposition or prepositions in the sentences below.**

1. The grin on Juan's face was bright and warm.

2. He greeted his cousin from Brazil with a smile and a handshake.

3. They walked through the airport and toward the baggage area.

4. Juan found his bags between two boxes.

5. The two cousins had not seen each other for five years.

6. They could spend hours talking about everything.

7. Juan and Luis got into Juan's truck.

8. Juan drove Luis to Juan's family's ranch.

9. It was a long ride across many hills and fields.

10. Luis rested his head against the seat.

11. Soon they drove over a hill and into a valley.

12. The ranch was located across the Harrison River.

13. The house stood among a group of oak trees.

14. Juan parked the truck beside the driveway.

15. They walked across the driveway and toward the house.

16. Juan's mother, Anita, stood behind the screen door.

17. Juan's family gathered around Luis.

18. Everyone sat on the porch and drank lemonade.

19. "Tell us about our relatives in Brazil," Rosa asked.

20. "You have over twenty cousins in my area," said Luis.

21. They go to school, just like you do.

22. Then everyone went into the house and ate dinner.

23. Juan's family passed the food across the table.

24. "Many of these dishes come from old family recipes," he said.

25. "It is wonderful to be among so many relatives," Luis said.

26. After dinner, everyone went to the living room.

27. Luis showed them photographs of his home in Brazil.

> ■ A **prepositional phrase** is a group of words that begins with a preposition and ends with a noun or pronoun.   EXAMPLE: Count the books **on the shelf.**
>
> ■ The noun or pronoun in a prepositional phrase is called the **object of the preposition.**   EXAMPLE: Count the books on the **shelf.**

■ **Put parentheses around each prepositional phrase. Then underline each preposition, and circle the object of the preposition.**

1. The founders (of the United States) had a vision (of a great country).

2. We climbed into the station wagon.

3. Many stars can be seen on a clear night.

4. The top of my desk has been varnished.

5. Have you ever gone through a tunnel?

6. Place these memos on the bulletin board.

7. We have a display of posters in the showcase in the corridor.

8. Carol, take these reports to Ms. Garza.

9. What is the capital of Alabama?

10. The fabric on this antique sofa came from France.

11. Are you a collector of minerals?

12. I am going to Julia's house.

13. The hillside was dotted with beautiful wild flowers.

14. The rain beat against the windowpanes.

15. We placed a horseshoe above the door.

16. This poem was written by my oldest sister.

17. Great clusters of grapes hung from the vine.

18. Is he going to the race?

19. A herd of goats grazed on the hillside.

20. Are you carrying those books to the storeroom?

21. Our car stalled on the bridge.

22. My family lives in St. Louis.

23. A small vase of flowers was placed in the center of the table.

24. The group sat around the fireplace.

25. The cold wind blew from the north.

26. Doris hit the ball over the fence.

27. The dog played with the bone.

28. High weeds grow by the narrow path.

Lesson
61
Prepositional Phrases as Adjectives/Adverbs

> ■ A prepositional phrase can be used to describe a noun or a pronoun.
> Then the prepositional phrase is being used as an **adjective** to tell
> which one, what kind, or how many.
> > EXAMPLE: The chair **in the corner** needs to be repaired.
> > The prepositional phrase <u>in the corner</u> tells **which** chair.
> ■ A prepositional phrase can be used to describe a verb. Then the
> prepositional phrase is being used as an **adverb** to tell how, where,
> or when.
> > EXAMPLE: Mrs. Porter repaired the chair **during the evening.**
> > The prepositional phrase <u>during the evening</u> tells **when** Mrs. Porter
> > repaired the chair.

■ **Underline the prepositional phrase in each sentence. Write <u>adjective</u> or <u>adverb</u> to tell
how the phrase is used.**

1. Sue went to the library. _____

2. She needed a book about gardening. _____

3. The shelves in the library contained many books. _____

4. She asked the librarian with blue shoes. _____

5. The librarian in the green dress was very helpful. _____

6. She taught Sue about the card catalog. _____

7. The card catalog has a card for every book. _____

8. The cards are organized in alphabetical order. _____

9. Some gardening books were in the health section. _____

10. Sue's trip to the library was a great success. _____

11. She took several books with her. _____

12. Sue read them at home. _____

13. The window seat in the living room was her favorite spot. _____

14. Sue looked out the window. _____

15. Her own garden by the backyard fence was dead. _____

16. The vegetables from last year's garden had been delicious. _____

17. She would plant more vegetables near the house. _____

18. Then she would have many vegetables in the summer. _____

Conjunctions

> - A **conjunction** is a word used to join words or groups of words.
>   EXAMPLES: Sally **and** Barb worked late. We worked **until** he arrived.
> - These are some commonly used conjunctions:
>
> | | | | | | | |
> |---|---|---|---|---|---|---|
> | although | because | however | or | that | until | whether |
> | and | but | if | since | though | when | while |
> | as | for | nor | than | unless | whereas | yet |
>
> - Some conjunctions are used in pairs. These include either . . . or, neither . . . nor, and not only . . . but also.

A. Underline each conjunction in the sentences below.

1. We waited until the mechanic replaced the part.

2. Plums and peaches are my favorite fruits.

3. The wind blew, and the rain fell.

4. Please call Alan or Grant for me.

5. A conjunction may connect words or groups of words.

6. Cotton and wheat are grown on nearby farms.

7. Neither Ann nor Bonnie is my cousin.

8. Their home is not large, but it is comfortable.

9. Ron and Sue arrived on time.

10. Do not move the vase, for you may drop it.

B. Complete each sentence with a conjunction.

1. I cannot leave _____ the baby-sitter arrives.

2. We must hurry, _____ we'll be late for work.

3. Battles were fought on the sea, on the land, _____ in the air.

4. Charles _____ Rick went to the movie, _____ Donald did not.

5. Please wait _____ Elizabeth gets ready.

6. Juan _____ I will carry that box upstairs.

7. Peter _____ Dan are twins.

8. We will stay home _____ you cannot go.

9. This nation exports cotton _____ wheat.

10. _____ the children _____ the parents liked the violent movie.

63 — Interjections

- An **interjection** is a word or group of words that expresses emotion.
  EXAMPLE: **Hurrah!** Our team has won the game.
- If the interjection is used to express sudden or strong feeling, it is followed by an exclamation mark.
  EXAMPLE: **Wow!** You've really done it this time.
- If the interjection is used to express mild emotion, it is followed by a comma.
  EXAMPLE: **Oh,** I see what you mean.
- These are some commonly used interjections:

ah	good grief	oh	ugh
aha	great	oops	well
alas	hurrah	sh	whew

■ **Write sentences with the following interjections.**

1. Ah _____

2. Wow _____

3. Oh _____

4. Ugh _____

5. Ouch _____

6. Oops _____

7. Hurrah _____

8. Oh no _____

9. Hey _____

10. Sh _____

11. Help _____

12. Well _____

13. Whew _____

14. Oh my _____

15. Hush _____

16. Hooray _____

17. Aha _____

18. Ha _____

A. Underline each common noun. Circle each proper noun.

1. John Madison is the president of companies in Dallas, Texas, and London, England.

2. Dr. Margaret Howe is a professor of business and economics at Jacksonville University.

3. Friends and relatives visiting our cabin on Lake Erie can enjoy swimming, fishing, boating, and hiking.

B. Write the plural form for each noun below.

_____ 1. magazine   _____ 4. potato

_____ 2. flash   _____ 5. elf

_____ 3. pony   _____ 6. stereo

C. Complete each sentence with the possessive form of the word in parentheses.

1. (parents) The _____ group held a book sale at the school.

2. (children) The _____ classes came at different times.

3. (teachers) All of the _____ favorite books were there.

4. (singers) The _____ voices blended perfectly together.

D. Underline the correct verb or the correct pronoun.

1. Have you (saw, seen) Matthew this morning?

2. Vince (did, done) all of the driving.

3. Maria (came, come) home a few minutes ago.

4. I (took, taken) my bicycle to the shop last Saturday.

5. Where has your friend (went, gone)?

6. I haven't (wrote, written) my invitations yet.

7. Gina (gave, given) her report yesterday.

8. It (don't, doesn't) take much time to walk to the store.

9. Where (was, were) you going yesterday?

10. Mark will go with Pam and (I, me) to visit Angela.

11. Beth and (I, me) signed up for music lessons.

12. Please take (we, us) with you when you go to the mall.

13. (They, Them) wanted to watch the Olympic Games on television.

14. (He, Him) was worried about finishing the test on time.

15. Give (they, them) those books and boxes.

E. Underline the correct pronouns in each sentence.

1. Mark will go with Pam and (I, me) to visit (us, our) friend Maria.

2. Beth and (I, me) will take singing lessons from (she, her).

3. Our friends will let (we, us) ride with (they, them).

4. (We, Us) will watch the Olympic Games at (their, they) house.

5. (He, Him) was worried that (her, she) would get lost.

6. (Who, Whom) is that woman with (he, him)?

7. It was (me, I) who found (him, his) dog.

8. She told the answer to (whom, who)?

F. Underline each adjective. Circle each adverb.

1. This short coat fit comfortably last year.

2. The large basket was filled with pink roses.

3. Many mistakes are caused by carelessness.

4. The fastest runners ran easily to the finish line.

5. She carefully followed the complicated directions of the new recipe.

G. Circle the correct form of each adjective or adverb.

1. Juan is the (youngest, younger) person to ever win a medal.

2. The neighbor's new dog barks (louder, loudest) than our dog.

3. The last singer in the talent show sang the (more beautifully, most beautifully) of all.

4. Jim swims (fastest, faster) than Paul.

5. She is (taller, tallest) than her brothers.

H. Underline the correct word in parentheses that completes each sentence.

1. Please (lie, lay) the books on the table.

2. I (don't, doesn't) understand your request.

3. You must (learn, teach) how to listen better.

4. Maybe you (may, can) tell me again.

5. Please (set, sit) down, and we'll talk.

6. I'd rather be (lying, laying) down.

7. It (don't, doesn't) matter what you are doing.

8. I will (learn, teach) you something you don't know.

I. Put parentheses around each prepositional phrase. Then underline each preposition and circle the object of the preposition.

1. Put this basket of clothes in the laundry room.

2. The hillside was covered with yellow daisies.

3. The top of the mountain is usually covered with snow.

4. The house on the corner was sold in one week.

A. Read the following paragraphs.

Christopher Columbus was born in the city of Genoa, Italy, around 1451. His father, a weaver, made cloth. Columbus learned many sailing skills because he grew up close to the sea. He worked on an Italian merchant ship and was shipwrecked on the rocky coast of Portugal. While he was in Portugal, he quickly learned new ways to build ships and to navigate. Columbus made several voyages along the African coast and even traveled as far north as Iceland.

Columbus first suggested the idea of sailing west to find a route to Japan and China to King John II of Portugal. The king was not interested, so Columbus went to the rulers of Spain, King Ferdinand and Queen Isabella. In 1492, the king and queen wisely granted their permission to Columbus and gave him three ships: the *Niña,* the *Pinta,* and the *Santa Maria.* Columbus set sail with a crew of ninety men.

B. In the paragraphs, find six common nouns, and write them on the lines below. Circle those that are plural.

1. _____   3. _____   5. _____

2. _____   4. _____   6. _____

C. Find six proper nouns, and write them on the lines below.

1. _____   3. _____   5. _____

2. _____   4. _____   6. _____

D. Find two proper adjectives and the nouns they describe, and write them on the lines below.

1. _____   2. _____

E. Find two adverbs and the verbs they describe, and write them on the lines below.

1. _____   2. _____

F. Find a sentence with an appositive, and write the sentence on the lines below.

_____

_____

G. Find six prepositional phrases, and write them on the lines below.

1. _____   4. _____

2. _____   5. _____

3. _____   6. _____

H. Rewrite the following paragraphs. Correct any mistakes in the use of nouns, pronouns, or verbs.

In 1585, a group of about 100 men come from England to Roanoke Island to sit up a colony. Them did not have enough food or supply's. The Native Americans was unfriendly. The group chosen to abandon the colony. In 1586, Sir Francis Drakes fleet stopped at the colony and took the men back to England.

The English people would not give up. In 1587, three ship left England. A group of 117 men, woman, and childrens settled on Roanoke Island. They expected to live on the supplies them received from England. In 1590, when the supply ships arriving in Roanoke, the colonists who had came in 1587 had disappeared. The people of Roanoke was never found. Their disappearance is a mysteries that has never been solved.

_____

_____

_____

_____

_____

_____

_____

_____

_____

_____

_____

_____

_____

_____

_____

_____

_____

_____

_____

> ■ **Capitalize** the first word of a sentence.
> EXAMPLE: Let's take a walk to the park.
> ■ Capitalize the first word of a quotation.
> EXAMPLE: Joseph said, "It's time for lunch."

A. Circle each letter that should be capitalized. Write the capital letter above it.

1. haven't you made an appointment to meet them?

2. the teenagers will go to the game together.

3. danielle asked, "how did she like the book?"

4. the family moved to another state last year.

5. "bring your scripts to the practice," said the director.

6. who wrote this article for the newspaper?

7. the woman said, "my party is in one week."

8. "have some more carrot sticks," said the host.

> ■ Capitalize the first word of every line of poetry.
> EXAMPLE: The strong winds whipped
> The sails of the ship
> ■ Capitalize the first, last, and all important words in the titles of books, poems, songs, and stories.
> EXAMPLES: *Gone with the Wind*   "America the Beautiful"

B. Circle each letter that should be capitalized. Write the capital letter above it.

1. i eat my peas with honey;

   i've done it all my life.

   it makes the peas taste funny,

   but it keeps them on the knife!

2. it's midnight, and the setting sun

   is slowly rising in the west;

   the rapid rivers slowly run,

   the frog is on his downy nest.

3. Who wrote the poem "the children's hour"?

4. My favorite novel is *a wrinkle in time.*

5. The high school band played "stand by me."

6. During the summer, Kim read *adam of the road.*

7. Carla gave her poem the title "chasing the wind."

> ■ Capitalize all **proper nouns.**
>   EXAMPLES: Sarah, Dad, Arbor Street, England, Maine, Arctic Ocean,
>   Ural Mountains, Columbus Day, February, Academy School, *Ocean Queen*
> ■ Capitalize all **proper adjectives.** A proper adjective is an adjective that
>   is made from a proper noun.
>   EXAMPLES: the Spanish language, American food, Chinese people

C. Rewrite the following paragraph. Be sure to add capital letters where they are needed.

chris and her friends went to a festival in chicago, illinois. Some of them tasted greek pastry and canadian cheese soup. charley thought that the italian sausage and mexican tacos were delicious! laurel tried an unusual japanese salad. They all watched some irish folk dancers and listened to german music.

_____

_____

_____

_____

_____

_____

_____

_____

_____

_____

D. Circle each letter that should be capitalized. Write the capital letter above it.

1. Did anita and her family drive through arizona, new mexico, and colorado?

2. Isn't brazil larger in area than the united states?

3. Did mark twain live in the small town of hannibal, missouri?

4. Have you read the story of martin luther king?

5. I have been reading about the solomon islands.

6. The north sea is connected with the english channel by the strait of dover.

7. At thirteen, sam houston moved to tennessee from lexington, virginia.

8. Isn't st. augustine the oldest city in the united states?

9. Is nairobi the capital of kenya?

10. Our friend brought japanese money back from her trip.

> - Capitalize a person's title when it comes before a name.
>   EXAMPLES: Doctor Baker, Governor Alvarez, Senator Washington
> - Capitalize abbreviations of titles.
>   EXAMPLES: Dr. Garcia, Supt. Barbara Shurna, Mr. J. Howell, Sr.

E. Circle each letter that should be capitalized. Write the capital letter above it.

1. Did captain cheng congratulate sergeant walters on his promotion?

2. The new health plan was developed by dr. ruth banks and mr. juan gomez.

3. After an introduction, pres. alice slater presented the next speaker, mr. allen norman.

4. When did principal grissom invite mayor hadley to attend the graduation ceremony?

5. Officer halpern was the first to stand up when judge patterson entered the courtroom.

6. How long has mrs. frank been working for president howell?

7. Does prof. mary schneider teach this course, or does dr. david towne?

8. Prince andrew of england will tour the southern states in the fall.

9. Senator alan howell is the uncle of supt. joyce randall.

> - Capitalize abbreviations of days and months, parts of addresses, and titles of members of the armed forces. Also capitalize all letters in abbreviations for states.
>   EXAMPLES: Fri., Jan., 3720 E. Franklin Ave., Gen. H. J. Farrimond, Los Angeles, CA, Dallas, TX

F. Circle each letter that should be capitalized. Write the capital letter above it.

1. capt. margaret k. hansen

   2075 lakeview st.

   phoenix, az 85072

2. jackson school Track Meet

   at wilson stadium

   tues., sept. 26, 10:30

   649 n. clark blvd.

3. mr. jonathan bernt

   150 telson rd.

   markham, ontario L3R 1E5

4. lt. gary l. louis

   5931 congress rd.

   syracuse, ny 13217

5. thanksgiving Concert

   wed., nov. 23, 11:00

   Practice tues., nov. 22, 3:30

   See ms. evans for details.

6. gen. david grimes

   329 n. hayes st.

   louisville, ky 40227

Using End Punctuation

> - Use a **period** at the end of a declarative sentence.
>   EXAMPLE: Theresa's aunt lives in Florida.
> - Use a **question mark** at the end of an interrogative sentence.
>   EXAMPLE: Will you carry this package for me?

A. Use a period or question mark to end each sentence below.

1. Ms. Clark has moved her law office____

2. Isn't this Dorothy's baseball glove____

3. Are you moving to Massachusetts next month____

4. It's too late to buy tickets for the game____

5. Our program will begin in five minutes____

6. Does your sister drive a truck____

7. Ms. Tobin's store was damaged by the flood____

8. Are you going to Rebecca's party____

9. Lucy did not take the plane to St. Petersburg____

10. Do you have a stamp for this envelope____

11. Have you ever seen Clarence laugh so hard____

12. President Sophia Harris called the meeting to order____

13. Will Gilmore Plumbing be open on Labor Day____

14. School ends the second week in June____

15. We are going camping in Canada this summer____

B. Add the correct end punctuation where needed in the paragraph below.

Have you ever been to the Olympic Games____ If not, have you ever seen them on television____ I hope to see them in person some day____ The Olympic Games are held every four years in a different country____ The games started in ancient Greece, but the games as we now know them date back to 1896____ Some of the finest athletes in the world compete for bronze, silver, and gold medals____ Can you think of a famous Olympic athlete____ What is your favorite Olympic sport____ It could be a winter or summer sport because the games are held for each season____ One American athlete won seven gold medals in swimming____ Can you imagine how excited that athlete must have felt, knowing that he had represented America so well____ That is the American record to date____ However, there will be plenty more chances for that record to be broken____

- Use a period at the end of an imperative sentence.
  EXAMPLE: Close the door to the attic.
- Use an **exclamation point** at the end of an exclamatory sentence and after an interjection that shows strong feelings.
  EXAMPLES: What a great shot! I'd love to go with you! Wow!

C. Add periods and exclamation points where needed in the sentences below.

1. Address the envelope to Dr. George K. Zimmerman____

2. How nicely dressed you are____

3. Hurry____ The bus is ready to leave____

4. Get some paints for your next art lesson____

5. Shake hands with Mr. D. B. Norton____

6. Oops____ I spilled the glass of orange juice____

7. Carry this bag to the car in the parking lot____

8. What a great view you have from your apartment window____

9. Wipe the counter when you're through eating____

10. Oh, what a beautiful painting____

11. I can't wait until summer vacation____

12. Please take this to the post office for me____

13. Just look at the size of the fish he caught____

14. I've never seen a larger one____

15. Get the net from under the life preserver____

16. I sure hope the pictures come out well____

D. Add the correct end punctuation where needed in the paragraph below.

    The state of Maine in New England is a wonderful place to visit in the summer or winter____ Have you ever been there____ It is best known for its rocky coastline on the Atlantic Ocean____ Visitors often drive along the rugged coast____ There are numerous quaint sea towns along the coast that date back to the 1600s____ What a long time ago that was____ Mount Katahdin and the northern part of the Appalachian Mountains are ideal places for winter sports, such as downhill and cross-country skiing____ If you've never seen a deer or moose, you'd probably see plenty of them while hiking in Acadia National Park____ It has over 30,000 acres____ Do you know anything about Maine's local fish____ Well, there are many kinds that are native to its rivers and lakes____ But Maine is famous for its Atlantic lobsters____ Rockport and Rockland are two of the largest cities for lobster fishing____ Lobsters from northern Maine are flown all over the world____ Blueberries are another big product of Maine____ Have you ever had wild blueberries____ Some people consider them to be the best____

> ■ Use a **comma** between words or groups of words in a series.
>   EXAMPLE: Be sure your business letter is brief, courteous, and correct.
> ■ Use a comma before a conjunction in a compound sentence.
>   EXAMPLE: Neal sketched the cartoon, and Clare wrote the caption.

A. Add commas where needed in the sentences below.

1. The United States exports cotton corn and wheat to many countries.

2. The children played softball ran races and pitched horseshoes.

3. Lauren held the nail and Tasha hit it with a hammer.

4. Alice Henry Carmen and James go to the library often.

5. The pitcher threw a fastball and the batter struck out.

6. Sara peeled the peaches and Victor sliced them.

7. The mountains were covered with forests of pine cedar and oak.

8. Craig should stop running or he will be out of breath.

9. Baseball is Lee's favorite sport but Sue's favorite is football.

10. Limestone marble granite and slate are found in Vermont New Hampshire and Maine.

11. The rain fell steadily and the lightning flashed.

12. Mindy enjoyed the corn but Frank preferred the string beans.

> ■ Use a comma to set off a quotation from the rest of a sentence.
>   EXAMPLES: "We must get up early," said Mom.
>   Mom said, "We must get up early."

B. Add commas before or after the quotations below.

1. "Please show me how this machine works" said Carolyn.

2. "Be sure you keep your eyes on the road" said the driving instructor.

3. Rick replied "I can't believe my ears."

4. Gail said "Travel is dangerous on the icy roads."

5. "Paul studied piano for two years" said Ms. Walters.

6. Alex said "That goat eats everything in sight."

7. "Let's go to the park for a picnic" said Marie.

8. "Wait for me here" said Paul.

9. Tom said "Sandra, thank you for the present."

10. "I'm going to the game with Al" remarked Frank.

11. Al asked "What time should we leave?"

12. Chris remembered "I was only five when we moved to New York."

> - Use a comma to set off the name of a person who is being addressed.
>   EXAMPLE: Betty, did you find the answer to your question?
> - Use a comma to set off words like yes, no, well, and oh at the beginning of a sentence.
>   EXAMPLE: No, I haven't seen Jack today.
> - Use a comma to set off an appositive.
>   EXAMPLE: Jack, Mary's brother, is going to college next fall.

C. Add commas where needed in the sentences below.

1. Miss Hunt do you know the answer to that question?

2. Can't you find the book I brought you last week Roger?

3. Dr. Levin the Smith's dentist sees patients on weekends.

4. Oh I guess it takes about an hour to get to Denver.

5. Joe may Sam and I go to the ball game?

6. Our neighbor Billy Johnson is a carpenter.

7. What is the population of your city Linda?

8. Well I'm not sure of the exact number.

9. Beth are you going skiing this weekend?

10. What time are you going to the concert Greg?

11. Joseph our friend coaches the softball team.

12. Sue have you seen a small black cat around your neighborhood?

13. Jeff do you know Mr. D. B. Norton?

14. No I don't think we've ever met.

15. Sally and John would you like to go shopping on Saturday?

16. Mrs. Porter the principal is retiring this year.

17. Yes the teachers are planning a retirement dinner for her.

18. Mrs. Porter and her husband Hal plan to move to Oregon.

D. Add commas where needed in the paragraph below.

I have two friends who are always there for me and I tell them everything. So it was a surprise to me when Carol my oldest friend said "Well when are you moving?" I said "What do you mean?" She said "I don't believe you our dearest friend wouldn't tell us first what was going on in your life." Margie my other friend said "I feel the same way. Ann why on earth did we have to hear about this from Ray?" "Margie and Carol I don't know what you're talking about" I said. "Oh don't be ashamed" said Margie. "We know you must have some good reason and we're waiting to hear it." "No I don't have any reason because I'm not moving" I said. "Ray that prankster must have been trying to play a joke on us" said Carol.

Using Quotation Marks and Apostrophes

■ Use **quotation marks** to show the exact words of a speaker. Use a comma or another punctuation mark to separate the quotation from the rest of the sentence.
> EXAMPLES: "Do you have a book on helicopters?" asked Tom.
> James said, "It's right here."

■ A quotation may be placed at the beginning or at the end of a sentence. It may also be divided within the sentence.
> EXAMPLES: Deborah said, "There are sixty active members."
> "Morton," asked Juanita, "have you read this magazine article?"

A. Add quotation marks and other punctuation where needed in the sentences below.

1. Dan, did you ever play football asked Tim.

2. Morris asked Why didn't you come in for an interview?

3. I have never said Laurie heard a story about a ghost.

4. Selina said Yuri thank you for the present.

5. When do we start on our trip to the mountains asked Stan.

6. Our guest said You don't know how happy I am to be in your house.

7. My sister said Kelly bought those beautiful baskets in Mexico.

8. I'm going to plant the spinach said Doris as soon as I get home.

■ Use an **apostrophe** in a contraction to show where a letter or letters have been taken out.
> EXAMPLES: Amelia **didn't** answer the phone. **I've** found my wallet.

■ Use an apostrophe to form a possessive noun. Add -'s to most singular nouns. Add -' to most plural nouns. Add -'s to a few nouns that have irregular plurals.
> EXAMPLES: A **child's** toy was in our yard. The **girls'** toys were in our yard. The **children's** toys were in our yard.

B. After each sentence below, write the word in which an apostrophe has been left out. Add the apostrophe where needed.

1. Many players uniforms are red. _____

2. That dog played with the babys shoe. _____

3. Julio isnt coming with us to the library. _____

4. Its very warm for a fall day. _____

5. The captains ship was one of the newest. _____

6. Marcia doesnt sing as well as my sister does. _____

7. Mens coats are sold in the new store. _____

Using Colons and Hyphens

- Use a **colon** after the greeting in a business letter.
  EXAMPLES: Dear Sir: Dear Ms. Franklin:
- Use a colon between the hour and the minute when writing time.
  EXAMPLES: 2:00   7:45   9:37
- Use a colon to introduce a list.
  EXAMPLE: The suitcase contained these items: a toothbrush, a brush, a comb, and some clothing.

A. Add colons where needed in the sentences or phrases below.

1. The program begins at 8 3 0.

2. Dear Mrs. Sanchez

3. These are the students who must return library books Julia Turner, Carl Porter, Crystal Fletcher, and Asako Satoshi.

4. Beverly wakes up every morning at 6 1 5.

5. Dear Mr. Graham

- Use a **hyphen** between the parts of some compound words.
  EXAMPLES: father-in-law   blue-black   well-known
             thirty-six   part-time   one-fourth
- Use a hyphen to separate the syllables of a word that is carried over from one line to the next.
  EXAMPLE: After eating dinner, we watched a television show about tor-nadoes in the Midwest.

B. Add hyphens where needed in the sentences below.

1. A driving safety expert will visit the school to give a presen tation on seat belts.

2. There should be forty two people at the lecture.

3. I searched high and low, but I couldn't seem to find that new, yellow zip per I bought today.

4. My mother in law is coming from Florida.

5. In fifty eight years of driving, he has a nearly perfect record.

6. Ralph and Victor came late to the meeting, but Lora and Angela arrived ear ly and stayed late.

7. George could lift weights with ease, and Alberto was able to swim twenty one laps without stopping.

8. Our air conditioning unit broke on the hottest day of this summer.

9. Donna had to go inside to change her clothes because Scoot, her frisky pup py, got his muddy paws on her.

■ **Circle each letter that should be capitalized. Write the capital letter above it. Place punctuation marks where needed.**

1. have you seen shelly today____

2. is major bill brandon your cousin____

3. mr. and mrs. john bell live at the mayflower apartments____

4. *alices adventures in wonderland* by lewis carroll is an

   excellent book ____

5. how do people travel in the deserts of egypt____

6. *heidi* was written by johanna spyri____

7. i cant wait to spend christmas in florida with uncle will and aunt lee____

8. monticello is the beautiful home of thomas jefferson near

   charlottesville, virginia____

9. *jungle book* was written by rudyard kipling____

10. florida produces more oranges than any other state in the united states____

11. i am sure she lives at 203 lincoln ave replied sandra____

12. mr. baldwin you won a trip to bermuda ____

13. the star spangled banner was written by francis scott key ____

14. mrs. perkins has written many interesting stories about the canadian

    alaskan and native american people ____

15. isnt mount everest the highest mountain in the world____

16. have you ever crossed the rocky mountains____

17. how many miles does the st. lawrence river flow____

18. one hundred french tourists were on the guided tour of washington, d.c____

19. sometime i want to visit mexico city____

20. carol r. brink wrote a book about a boy in scotland____

21. the first monday in september is known as labor day____

22. the olympic team will leave for paris, france, on thanksgiving day____

B. Add commas where needed in the sentences below.

1. Tom do you know where the paper pencils and test forms are?

2. "We really enjoyed our trip through Florida Georgia and South Carolina" said
   Mr. Shaw.

3. I gave Angela my niece a pair of skates for her birthday and her parents gave
   her a radio.

4. "Jason please wash dry and fold the laundry for me" said Connie.

5. Dr. Wells our family doctor is retiring but Dr. Hernandez will take over her
   practice.

6. Yes I think Ms. Lawson my supervisor is a courteous capable and fair person.

7. I want to go to the beach on our vacation but my friend wants to go camping
   hiking and fishing.

8. Do you want to go to a movie or play cards Sharonda?

9. Mr. Coe my English instructor said "Make sure your reports are neat concise
   and accurate."

10. Dawn told Ms. Mendez a nurse about Kelsey's fever.

11. James will mow the yard trim the hedge and water the flowers.

12. Sara Powell the district attorney will look into the case.

C. Add quotation marks, apostrophes, colons, or hyphens where needed in the sentences below.

1. My mother in law said, Marys aunt will join us for dinner at 730.

2. Rosa couldnt find the following items for her trip suntan lotion, her hat, and
   the keys to the cabin.

3. Juan, asked Linda, will you please bring forty eight cookies for the clubs
   bake sale?

4. Ms. Tysons secretary began the letter with Dear Sir I am writing on behalf of
   Ms. Tyson.

5. Scott said, Im going to Jims house tonight at 800 to help him finish his sons desk.

6. Megs friends gave her many gifts at her good bye party a new shirt, two headbands,
   stationery, and a roll of stamps.

7. Mike and Todd dont have to go to bed until 930, said Larry.

8. Mr. Reids son is only twenty one years old and is already a well known figure in the com
   munity.

9. Rita said, The beautiful memorial fountain is near the parks main entrance.

10. Wont you be taking the coachs extra credit class? asked Eric.

11. Stephanies party begins at 830.

12. What time is your appointment, Jack? asked Diane.

A. Correct the stories below. Circle each letter that should be capitalized. Add missing periods, question marks, exclamation points, commas, quotation marks, colons, apostrophes, or hyphens where needed. Be sure to write the correct end punctuation on the blank after each sentence.

one of aesops fables is called "the fox and the crow＿＿" it tells about a crow that stole a piece of cheese＿＿ the crow landed on the branch of a tree put the cheese in her mouth and began to eat it＿＿ but a fox was also interested in the cheese＿＿ he sat under the branch and he thought about eating the cheese, too＿＿

the fox said crow i compliment you on your size beauty and strength＿＿ you would be the queen of all birds if you had a voice＿＿

caw exclaimed the crow＿＿

well the crow dropped the cheese＿＿ the fox pounced on it carried it off a few feet and then turned around＿＿

my friend said the fox you have every good quality except common sense＿＿

---

our neighbor denise baldwin likes to tell me funny stories＿＿ one hot friday afternoon in august she told me about her trip to atlanta, georgia＿＿ she was walking out of a store with some presents she had bought for pat her sister＿＿ they were three joke gifts which included the following birthday candles that didnt blow out a silly hat and a mustache attached to some glasses＿＿ denise accidentally bumped into another shopper＿＿

im so sorry exclaimed denise＿＿

are you hurt asked the other shopper＿＿

no im not hurt said denise＿＿ both shoppers had dropped their presents and they bent over to pick them up＿＿

im denise baldwin she said as she picked up the presents＿＿

my name is carol schwartz said the other shopper＿＿

both shoppers said they were sorry again and then went on their way＿＿

denise gave her sister the presents when she returned to miami, florida＿＿ pat had a puzzled look on her face when she unwrapped them＿＿ the packages contained a rattle a bib and a baby bonnet＿＿

oh gasped denise i must have picked up the wrong presents when i bumped into ms. schwartz＿＿

whos ms. schwartz asked pat＿＿

denise laughed and said i hope shes someone who likes joke gifts＿＿

B. Rewrite the story below. Be sure to use capital letters and punctuation marks where they are needed.

sir walter scott one of the worlds greatest storytellers was born in
edinburgh, scotland, on august 15, 1771____ walter had an illness just before
he was two years old that left him lame for the rest of his life____ his par
ents were worried so they sent him to his grandparents farm in sandy
knowe____ they thought the country air would do him good____

walters parents were right____ he was quite healthy by the time he was six
years old____ he was happy, too____ walter loved listening to his grandfather
tell stories about scotland____ the stories stirred his imagination____ he began
to read fairy tales travel books and history books____ it was these ear
ly stories that laid the groundwork for Scotts later interest in writing stories____
his most famous book *Ivanhoe* has been read by people around the
world____

Writing Sentences

> - Every sentence has a base consisting of a simple subject and a simple predicate.
>   EXAMPLE: <u>Dolphins</u> <u>leap</u>.
> - Expand the meaning of a sentence by adding adjectives, adverbs, and prepositional phrases to the sentence base.
>   EXAMPLE: **The sleek** dolphins **suddenly** leap **high into the air.**

A. Expand the meaning of each sentence base by adding adjectives, adverbs, and/or prepositional phrases. Write each expanded sentence.

1. (Dinner cooks.) _____

2. (Clown chuckled.) _____

3. (Car raced.) _____

4. (Dancer spun.) _____

5. (Panthers growled.) _____

6. (Leaves fall.) _____

7. (Bread baked.) _____

8. (Lake glistened.) _____

9. (Ship glides.) _____

B. Write five sentence bases. Then write an expanded sentence containing each sentence base.

1. _____

   _____

2. _____

   _____

3. _____

   _____

4. _____

   _____

5. _____

   _____

Lesson 70

Writing Topic Sentences

■ A **topic sentence** is the sentence within a paragraph that states the
main idea. It is often placed at the beginning of a paragraph.

EXAMPLE:

The trip to the national park was a great success. First, the
visitors learned a lot from their guide about the park. They learned
that the forest was created by people, not by nature. To their surprise,
they found out that the park had more than five hundred species of
plants. Then they went on a hike and even spotted a falcon flying
overhead. Finally, the visitors had a wonderful picnic lunch and
headed back home.

A. Write a topic sentence for each paragraph below.

1.   Some jewelry is made out of feathers, leather, shells, or wood. Other jewelry
is crafted from gold, silver, brass, copper, or other metals. Gems and unusual
stones are added for their beauty and value.

    Topic Sentence: _____

2.   A pet goldfish needs clean water. A pump should be placed in the water to
supply fresh air. The water temperature must be constant, and it must not go
below 27°C (80°F). The goldfish should be fed flaked fish food or small insects.

    Topic Sentence: _____

3.   When Jana crawls over to a kitchen cabinet, she whips the door open to
see what's behind it. With a little help from Jana, the pots and pans are on
the floor in no time. If she sees a bag of groceries, Jana has to investigate
the contents. After she is tucked in bed for the night, this toddler loves to
climb out of her crib and explore.

    Topic Sentence: _____

B. Write a topic sentence for each of the paragraph ideas below.

1. birthday parties _____

2. a great adventure _____

3. a great president _____

4. a favorite holiday _____

5. homework _____

6. video games _____

7. vacations _____

8. the Olympics _____

100

Unit 5, Composition

Writing Supporting Details

> ■ The idea expressed in a topic sentence can be developed with sentences containing **supporting details**. Details can include facts, examples, and reasons.

A. Read the topic sentence below. Then read the sentences that follow. Circle the seven sentences that contain details that support the topic sentence.

Topic Sentence: The Big Dipper Theme Park is a wonderful place to go for a fun-filled day.

1. The roller coaster is the most popular ride in the park.

2. The park was built in 1959.

3. You can test your pitching skills at the game booths.

4. You can win a stuffed animal at one of the pitching games.

5. Young children can enjoy a part of the park made especially for them.

6. We had sandwiches and potato salad for lunch.

7. The train ride is a pleasant way to relax and see the park.

8. However, the water rides are a great way to beat the heat.

9. What do you like to do during summer vacation?

10. The sky ride provides a grand tour of the park from high in the air.

B. Choose one of the topic sentences below. Write it on the first line. Then write five sentences that contain supporting details. The details can be facts, examples, or reasons.

1. Exercise is important for maintaining good health.

2. Being the oldest child in a family has its advantages.

3. The teen-age years are a time of change.

4. True friendship makes life more interesting and fun.

_____

_____

_____

_____

_____

_____

_____

_____

Topic and Audience

> - The **topic** of a paragraph is the subject of the paragraph.
> - The **title** of a paragraph should be based on the topic.
> - The **audience** is the person or persons who will read the paragraph.
>   EXAMPLES: teachers, classmates, readers of the school newspaper, friends, family members

A. Suppose that you chose the topic <u>watching TV</u>. Underline the sentence that you would choose for the topic sentence.

1. Watching TV is one of the best ways to learn about things.

2. Watching TV is a waste of time.

3. The time children spend watching TV should be limited.

B. Think about the topic sentence you chose in Exercise A. Then underline the audience for whom you would like to write.

1. your friends

2. your family members

3. readers of a newspaper

C. Write a paragraph beginning with the topic sentence you chose in Exercise A. Keep your audience in mind as you write. Be sure to write a title.

_____

> - **Note-taking** is an important step when writing a report.
> - You can find information for reports in encyclopedias, books, and magazines.
> - Before you begin, organize your research questions.
> - Write information accurately and in your own words.
> - Take more notes than you expect to need, so you won't have to go back to your sources a second time.

A. Underline a topic below that interests you.

1. a favorite hobby
2. the stars or planets
3. a historical figure
4. a species of animal
5. movies

6. a favorite sport
7. a favorite food
8. fashion or costumes
9. gardening
10. airplanes

B. Gather some sources of information about your topic. Write the name of your topic on the first line below. For example, if you have chosen "a favorite food," you might write the name of that particular food. Then write notes about the topic on the remaining lines.

_____

_____

_____

_____

_____

_____

_____

_____

_____

_____

_____

Outlining

■ Organize your thoughts before writing by making an **outline.** An outline consists of the title of the topic, **main headings** for the main ideas, and **subheadings** for the supporting ideas.

■ Main headings are listed after Roman numerals. Subheadings are listed after capital letters.

Topic: First aid for burns

Main heading   I. Keeping the wound clean

Subheadings {   A. Applying thick, clean dressing
B. Avoiding sprays or oils

II. Easing pain
A. Applying ice packs
B. Putting injured area in ice water

■ **Write an outline for the topic you chose in Exercise A on page 103. Use the sample outline as a guide.**

Topic: _____

I. _____

   A. _____

   B. _____

II. _____

   A. _____

   B. _____

III. _____

   A. _____

   B. _____

IV. _____

   A. _____

   B. _____

V. _____

   A. _____

   B. _____

Writing a Report

■ A **report** is a series of informative paragraphs covering a main topic. Each paragraph has a topic sentence and other sentences that contain supporting details. Begin with a paragraph that introduces the report, and end with a paragraph that concludes the report.

A. Read the paragraphs below.

Exploring the Mystery Planets: Uranus, Neptune, and Pluto

The planets Uranus, Neptune, and Pluto are difficult to study because of their distance from Earth. However, scientists are not completely without information about these planets. They know, for example, that Uranus is more than twice as far from Earth as Saturn is. They also know that Neptune is half again as far from Earth as Uranus. Both Saturn and Uranus are four times the size of Earth.

Scientists have explored the mysteries of Uranus. As Uranus orbits the sun every 84 years, it rolls around on its side. Although it is larger than Earth and orbits the sun more slowly, Uranus spins on its axis very rapidly. It completes a full rotation in 15 hours, 30 minutes. Five known satellites accompany Uranus, along with a system of nine dark rings that were discovered in 1977. The diameter of Uranus is 32,500 miles (52,200 kilometers), and the planet lies 1.78 billion miles (2.87 billion kilometers) from the sun. Because of this great distance, the temperature of Uranus is −360°F (−220°C), far too cold for any earth creature to survive.

Scientists have also explored the mysteries of Neptune. At a distance of 2.8 billion miles (4.5 billion kilometers) from the sun, Neptune appears through a telescope as a greenish-blue disc. Neptune is somewhat smaller than Uranus, having a diameter of about 30,000 miles. It is also very cold (−328°F, or −200°C). Two of Neptune's satellites have been named Nereid and Triton. In the summer of 1989, *Voyager 2* finally passed Neptune and, among other things, revealed that there are up to five rings around the planet.

It was 1930 before Pluto, the last planet in our solar system, was discovered. The "new" planet is 3.67 billion miles (6 billion kilometers) from the sun and takes 248 years to complete its orbit. In comparison, Earth takes only 365 days to complete a single orbit. While Pluto has not been measured exactly, scientists believe that it has a diameter of 1,600 miles (2,670 kilometers).

There are more interesting facts about Pluto. It also has a satellite, called Charon, which is five times closer to Pluto than our moon is to Earth. The yellowish color of Pluto indicates that it has very little atmosphere. Pluto's distance from the sun indicates that its climate is the coldest of the nine planets in our solar system.

Many mysteries remain concerning Uranus, Neptune, and Pluto, despite the fact that so much has been discovered. The questioning minds of the twenty-first century will continue our search for the secrets of space.

B. Circle the word or phrase that best completes each statement about this report.

1. Most of the report's supporting details are (facts, examples, reasons).

2. The writer of this report has included the (color, discoverer, diameter) of each of the three planets.

3. The writer does not discuss the relationship of the mystery planets to (Earth, Mars, the sun).

C. Underline the topic sentence in each paragraph.

- **Revising** gives you a chance to rethink and review what you have written and to improve your writing. Revise by adding words and information, by taking out unneeded words and information, and by moving words, sentences, and paragraphs around.
- **Proofreading** has to do with checking spelling, punctuation, grammar, and capitalization. Use proofreader's marks to show changes needed in your writing.

Proofreader's Marks

≡	⊙	⑤ⓟ
Capitalize.	Add a period.	Correct spelling.
/	∧	⌐H
Make a small letter.	Add something.	Indent for new paragraph.
∧	℘	⟶
Add a comma.	Take something out.	Move something.

A. Rewrite the paragraph below. Correct the errors by following the proofreader's marks.

⌐H yellowstone national park is the oldest and largest park national in the united

states. It is located partly in northwestern wyoming, partly in southern montana, and

partley in easturn idaho idaho. during the summur large parts of park the were

damaged by fire. A serious lack of rein was part of the reason the fire was sew

severe. one fire threatened almost to destroy the park's famous lodge, which is

constructed entirely of wood. fortunately, firefighters' efforts saved the lodge from

desturction. today the forests are slowly recovering from the fires.

_____

_____

_____

_____

_____

_____

_____

B. Read the paragraphs below. Use proofreader's marks to revise and proofread the paragraphs. Then write your revised paragraphs below.

although yellowstons national park is the largest national national park in the United states, other national parks are also well-known yosemite national park in california has acres of Mountain Scenery and miles of hiking trails. Won of the world's largest biggest waterfalls can also be found in yosemite.

mammoth cave national park in kentucky features a huge underground cave the cave over has 212 miles of corridors it also have underground lakes rivers and waterfalls this cave system is estimated to be millions of years old

many pepul are surprized to learn that their are national parks in alaska and hawaii. mount McKinley the highest mountain in north america is located in denali national park in alaska. you can travel to hawaii and visit hawaii volcanoes national park this Park Has too active volcanoes rare plants and animals.

_____

_____

_____

_____

_____

_____

_____

_____

_____

_____

_____

_____

Writing a Business Letter

■ A **business letter** has six parts.
- The **heading** contains the address of the person writing and the date.
- The **inside address** contains the name and address of the person to whom the letter is written.
- The **greeting** tells to whom the letter is written. Use "Dear Sir or Madam" if you are unsure who will read the letter. Use a colon after the greeting in a business letter.
- The **body** is the message of the letter. It should be brief, courteous, and to the point.
- The **closing** is the ending that follows the body.
- The **signature** is the name of the person who is writing the letter.

■ When writing a business letter, remember the following:
- Use business-size paper and envelopes.
- Center your letter on the page, leaving at least a one-inch margin on each side.
- Include specific information, such as quantities, sizes, numbers, brands, prices, manner of shipment, and amount of payment.
- When you have finished, reread your letter. Rewrite it if you are not satisfied with any part of it.

A. Study this business letter. Then answer the questions below.

heading	572 Ironwood Avenue Orlando, FL 32887 April 4, 1994
inside address	Order Department Perfection Computer Company 9940 Main Street Brooklyn, NY 11227

greeting
body
	Dear Sir or Madam:
	    Please send me one copy of <u>Making Friends With Your Computer</u>. Enclosed is $16.95 to cover the cost of the book plus shipping and handling.
	    Thank you for your assistance.

closing	Sincerely yours,
signature	*Chris Morrow* Chris Morrow

1. Who wrote the letter? _____

2. What is the greeting? _____

3. Where is Perfection Computer Company located? _____

_____

4. When was the letter written? _____

- Use a business-size envelope for a business letter. Be sure to include your return address. Check both addresses to be sure they are correct.

Chris Morrow
572 Ironwood Avenue
Orlando, FL 32887

Order Department
Perfection Computer Company
9940 Main Street
Brooklyn, NY 11227

B. Write a brief business letter asking for information about the Chicago Fire that you can use in a report. Write to the Chicago Historical Society at 1601 North Clark Street in Chicago, Illinois. The zip code is 60616. Then circle the parts of the letter that would appear on the envelope.

A. Write expanded sentences by adding adjectives, adverbs, and/or prepositional phrases to each sentence below.

1. (Whistle blew.) _____

2. (Calvary rode.) _____

3. (Fire trucks roared.) _____

B. Write a possible topic sentence for each topic below.

1. friendship _____

2. zoos _____

C. Write a topic sentence for each paragraph below.

1. Trees provide shade from the sun and block the wind. They provide homes and food for many animals. Trees are the source of wood for thousands of useful products.

Topic Sentence: _____

2. Dogs help police officers find criminals and illegal substances. They guard homes and businesses. Some dogs help disabled people live more independent lives.

Topic Sentence: _____

D. Circle the letters for the sentences that contain details that support the topic sentences below.

1. Topic Sentence: Rockets have many peacetime uses.

a. They are used to signal that a ship is in trouble.

b. High-performance rockets must have large nozzles.

c. Rockets carry cables across rivers for the construction of bridges.

2. Topic Sentence: Computers are very useful in schools.

a. They are used to help students practice reading, writing, and math skills.

b. Teachers keep records on computers.

c. Computers can be used to store a great deal of information.

3. Topic Sentence: Our first camping trip was a disaster.

a. We all got poison ivy while fishing in a nearby stream.

b. We set up our tents in a camping area.

c. Our campground had to be evacuated because of a large brushfire.

E. Read the following paragraphs. Take notes, and make an outline from the information.

The Moon

The moon is Earth's closest neighbor in space. It is about 239,000 miles away. The moon is about one-fourth the size of the earth. It has a diameter of about 2,160 miles.

The moon is always moving in space. It revolves around Earth in an oval path. The moon completes one revolution in about 27 1/3 days. The moon also rotates, or turns on its axis, as it revolves around the earth. It take one month for the moon to revolve around Earth.

Notes

_____

_____

_____

Outline

I. _____

    A. _____

    B. _____

    C. _____

II. _____

    A. _____

    B. _____

F. Find ten spelling, punctuation, and grammar errors in the paragraph below. Use the proofreader's marks on page 102 to mark the errors.

Flying a kite can be fun, but it can also serve some practical purposes. For example, Benjamin franklin uses a kite in his experiments with electricity. In the early part of the twentieth century, box kites carring instruments measured wind speed temperature pressure and and humidity. they were also used to lift soldiers to hieghts where they could see the enemy. Today they serve as signals in air-see-rescue operations.

G. Number the six parts of a business letter in the order in which they appear in a letter.

_____ 1. body   _____ 3. heading   _____ 5. greeting

_____ 2. closing   _____ 4. inside address   _____ 6. signature

A. Write a report about the topic you chose on page 103. Use your outline and notes in writing the report. Be sure to write an interesting topic sentence for each paragraph and to use supporting details. Keep your audience in mind as you write. You may use the report on page 101 as a model. You might need to use your own paper.

_____

_____

_____

_____

_____

_____

_____

_____

_____

_____

_____

_____

_____

_____

_____

_____

_____

_____

_____

B. Proofread and revise the report you wrote on page 112. Write your revised report below. You might need to use your own paper.

- A **dictionary** is a reference book that contains definitions of words and other information about their history and use.
- **Entries** in a dictionary are listed in **alphabetical order.**
- **Guide words** appear at the top of each dictionary page. Guide words show the first and last entry on the page.
  EXAMPLE: The word dog would appear on a dictionary page with the guide words dodge / doll. The word dull would not.

A. Put a check in front of each word that would be listed on the dictionary page with the given guide words.

1. frozen / gather	2. money / muscle	3. perfect / pin
_____ fruit	_____ muddy	_____ perfume
_____ grain	_____ moss	_____ pit
_____ furnish	_____ motorcycle	_____ pick
_____ gate	_____ mustard	_____ photo
_____ gallon	_____ moisten	_____ pest
_____ former	_____ moose	_____ plastic
_____ forgive	_____ museum	_____ pillow
_____ fuzz	_____ morning	_____ pile
_____ galaxy	_____ mortal	_____ pipe
_____ future	_____ modest	_____ pizza

B. Number the words in each column in the order in which they would appear in a dictionary. Then write the words that could be the guide words for each column.

1. _____ / _____	2. _____ / _____	3. _____ / _____
_____ raccoon	_____ seize	_____ octopus
_____ radar	_____ shellfish	_____ olive
_____ rabbit	_____ shrink	_____ of
_____ raisin	_____ signal	_____ office
_____ react	_____ silent	_____ old
_____ reflect	_____ scent	_____ odor
_____ rebel	_____ shuffle	_____ once
_____ rainfall	_____ shaft	_____ oil
_____ relay	_____ serpent	_____ odd
_____ remind	_____ seldom	_____ onion
_____ refuse	_____ scope	_____ occasion
_____ ran	_____ selfish	_____ only

Dictionary: Syllables

> ■ A **syllable** is a part of a word that is pronounced at one time. Dictionary
> entry words are divided into syllables to show how they can be divided
> at the end of a writing line.
> ■ A **hyphen (-)** is placed between syllables to separate them.
>   EXAMPLE: man-a-ger
> ■ If a word has a beginning or ending syllable of only one letter, do not
> divide it so that one letter stands alone.
>   EXAMPLES: a-lone   sand-y

A. Write each word as a whole word.

1. ad-ver-tise _____

2. blun-der _____

3. par-a-dise _____

4. mis-chie-vous _____

5. con-crete _____

6. mi-cro-phone _____

7. in-ci-dent _____

8. val-ue _____

B. Find each word in a dictionary. Rewrite the word, placing a hyphen between each syllable.

1. bicycle _____

2. solution _____

3. category _____

4. punishment _____

5. behavior _____

6. quarterback _____

7. disappear _____

8. theory _____

9. wonderful _____

10. biology _____

11. sizzle _____

12. foreign _____

13. transparent _____

14. civilization _____

C. Write two ways in which each word may be divided at the end of a writing line.

1. mosquito _____mos-quito_____   _____mosqui-to_____

2. ambition _____   _____

3. boundary _____   _____

4. gingerbread _____   _____

5. geography _____   _____

6. leadership _____   _____

Dictionary: Pronunciation

> ■ Each dictionary entry word is followed by a respelling that shows how the word is **pronounced.**
> ■ **Accent marks** (′) show which syllable or syllables are said with extra stress.
>   EXAMPLE: hope-ful (hōp′ fəl)
> ■ A **pronunciation key** (shown below) explains the other symbols used in the respellings.

A. Use the pronunciation key to answer the questions.

1. Which word contains an a that is pronounced the same

   as the a in apple? _____

2. How many words are given for the symbol ə? _____

3. Think of another word that contains the sound of ə.

   _____

> at; āpe; fär; câre; end; mē; it; īce; pîerce; hot; ōld; sông; fôrk; oil; out; up; ūse; rüle; pu̇ll; tûrn; chin; sing; shop; thin; <u>th</u>is; hw in white; zh in treasure. The symbol ə stands for the unstressed vowel sound in about, taken, pencil, lemon, and circus.

4. What symbol represents the sound of the wh in whether? _____

5. What is the symbol for the pronunciation of oo in boot? _____

6. What is the symbol for the pronunciation of th in themselves? _____

B. Use the pronunciation key to help you choose the correct word for each respelling. Underline the correct word.

1. (ə līv′)   olive   live   alive
2. (lōd)   load   lead   loud
3. (trōō)   threw   true   try
4. (thik)   thick   trick   tick
5. (fôl ən)   fallen   falling   fooling
6. (kāp)   cap   cop   cape
7. (īs)   is   ice   as
8. (<u>th</u>ā) that   they   the
9. (sup′ ər)   super   support   supper
10. (lok′ ər)   locker   looker   lock
11. (hōm)   hum   hem   home
12. (fôt)   fought   fat   fit
13. (mīt)   mitt   meet   might
14. (fül)   full   fuel   fool
15. (frēz)   froze   free   freeze
16. (let′ is)   lettuce   let's   less

Dictionary: Definitions and Parts of Speech

- A dictionary lists the **definitions** of each entry word. Many words have more than one definition. In this case, the most commonly used definition is given first. Sometimes a definition is followed by a sentence showing a use of the entry word.
- A dictionary also gives the **part of speech** for each entry word. An abbreviation (shown below) stands for each part of speech. Some words might be used as more than one part of speech.

   EXAMPLE: **frost** (frôst) *n.* **1.** frozen moisture. *There was frost on all the leaves. -v.* **2.** to cover with frosting. *I'll frost the cake when it's cool.*

- **Use the dictionary samples below to answer the questions.**

spec-i-fy (spes′ ə fī′) *v.* **1.** to say or tell in an exact way: *Please specify where we should meet you.* **2.** to designate as a specification: *The artist specified brown for the frame.*

spec-i-men (spes′ ə mən) *n.* **1.** a single person or thing that represents the group to which it belongs; example. **2.** a sample of something taken for medical purposes.

speck-le (spek′ əl) *n.* a small speck or mark. *-v.* to mark with speckles.

spec-tac-u-lar (spek tak′ yə lər) *adj.* relating to, or like a spectacle. *-n.* an elaborate show. —spec tac′ u lar ly, *adv.*

1. Which word can be used as either a noun

   or a verb? _____

2. Which word can be used only as a verb?

   _____

3. Which word can be used only as a noun?

   _____

n.	noun
pron.	pronoun
v.	verb
adj.	adjective
adv.	adverb
prep.	preposition

4. Which word can be used either as a noun or as an adjective? _____

5. Write a sentence using the first definition of spectacular. _____

   _____

6. Write a sentence using the first definition of specify. _____

   _____

7. Write a sentence using speckle as a verb. _____

   _____

8. Use the second definition of specimen in a sentence. _____

   _____

9. Which word shows an adverb form? _____

10. Which word shows two definitions used as a noun? _____

Dictionary: Word Origins

> ■ An **etymology** is the origin and development of a word. Many dictionary
> entries include etymologies. The etymology is usually enclosed in
> brackets [ ].
>
> EXAMPLE: **knit** [ME *knitten* < OE *cnyttan*, to knot]. The word *knit*
> comes from the Middle English word *knitten,* which came from the
> Old English word *cnyttan,* meaning "to tie in a knot."

■ **Use these dictionary entries to answer the questions.**

cam-pus (kam′ pəs) *n.* the grounds and buildings of a school
or university. [Latin *campus,* meaning field, perhaps
because most colleges used to be in the country.]

chaise longue (shāz lông′) *n.* a chair with a long seat which
supports the sitter's outstretched legs. [French *chaise,* chair
+ *longue,* long.]

gar-de-nia (gär dēn′ yə) *n.* a fragrant yellow or white flower
from an evergreen shrub or tree. [Modern Latin *Gardenia,*
from Alexander *Garden,* 1730–1791, U.S. scientist who
studied plants.]

pas-teur-ize (pas′ chə rīz) *v.* to heat food to a high
temperature in order to destroy harmful bacteria. [From
Louis *Pasteur,* inventor of the process.]

rent (rent) *n.* a regular payment for the use of property.
[Old French *rente,* meaning taxes.]

ut-ter (ut′ ər) *v.* to express; make known; put forth. [From
Middle English or Dutch, *utteren,* literally, out.]

wam-pum (wom′ pəm) *n.* small beads made from shells
and used for money or jewelry. [Short for Algonquin
wampompeag, meaning strings of money.]

1. Which word comes from an Algonquin word? _____

2. What does the Algonquin word mean? _____

3. Which word was formed from the name of an inventor? _____

4. Which word comes from French words? _____

5. What do the French words <u>chaise</u> and <u>longue</u> mean? _____

6. Which word was formed from the name of a scientist? _____

7. Which word is short for the word <u>wampompeag</u>? _____

8. Which words come from Latin words? _____

9. Which word comes from a Middle English word? _____

10. What does the French word <u>rente</u> mean? _____

11. Which word comes from two languages? _____

12. What does the word <u>utteren</u> mean? _____

13. What does the Latin word <u>campus</u> mean? _____

14. Which word is the name of a flower? _____

15. Which word names a piece of furniture? _____

Using Parts of a Book

> - A **title page** lists the name of a book and its author.
> - A **copyright page** tells who published the book, where it was published, and when it was published.
> - A **table of contents** lists the chapter or unit titles and the page numbers on which they begin. It is at the front of a book.
> - An **index** gives a detailed list of the topics in a book and the page numbers on which each topic is found. It is in the back of a book.

A. Answer the questions below.

1. Where would you look to find when a book was published? _____

2. Where would you look to find the page number of a particular topic? _____

3. Where would you look to find the author's name? _____

4. Where would you look to find the titles of the chapters in a book? _____

B. Use your *Language Exercises* book to answer the questions.

1. When was this book published? _____

2. Who is the publisher? _____

3. Where is the publishing company located? _____

4. On what page does Unit 6 begin? _____

5. On what page does the lesson on nouns begin? _____

6. What lesson begins on page 104? _____

7. What pages teach capitalization? _____

8. What page teaches indefinite pronouns? _____

9. What lesson begins on page 6? _____

10. What is the name of Unit 1? _____

11. What is the title of lesson 24? _____

12. On what page does Unit 2 begin? _____

13. What is the name of Unit 6? _____

14. On what page does the Unit 5 Review begin? _____

15. What is the title of lesson 38? _____

- Books on library shelves are arranged by **call numbers.** Each book is assigned a number from 000 to 999, according to its subject matter.
- The main subject groups for call numbers are as follows:

000–099 Reference	500–599 Science and Math
100–199 Philosophy	600–699 Technology
200–299 Religion	700–799 The Arts
300–399 Social Sciences	800–899 Literature
400–499 Languages	900–999 History and Geography

A. Write the call number group in which you would find each book.

1. *A Guide to Electronics in a New Age* _____

2. *A Traveler's Handbook of Everyday German* _____

3. *1994 World Almanac and Book of Facts* _____

4. *A History of the Roman Empire* _____

5. *The Modern Philosophers* _____

6. *Religions of the World* _____

7. *Solving Word Problems in Mathematics* _____

8. *Folktales of Norway* _____

9. *Painting with Watercolors* _____

10. *People in Society* _____

11. *Learn Spanish in Seven Days* _____

12. *Science Experiments for the Beginner* _____

13. *Technology in a New Century* _____

14. *Funny Poems for a Rainy Day* _____

15. *The Continent of Africa* _____

B. Write the titles of three of your favorite books. Write the call number group beside each title.

1. _____

2. _____

3. _____

Using the Card Catalog

> - The **card catalog** contains information cards on every book in the library. Some libraries are now computerized and have no card catalogs. But the information in the computer is filed in the same manner as the information in the card catalog.
> - Each book has three cards in the catalog. They are filed separately according to:
>   1. the author's last name
>   2. the subject of the book
>   3. the title of the book

A. Use the sample catalog card to answer the questions.

Author Card

Call number — 920.067 H66

Hoobler, Dorothy and Thomas — Author

Title — Images across the ages: African portraits; illustrated by

John Gampert. – Austin : Raintree/Steck-Vaughn — Publisher

Austin — Place published

Date published — ©1993

Number of pages — 96 p. : illus. — Illustrated

1. What are the authors' names? _____

2. What is the title of the book? _____

3. How many pages does the book have? _____

4. What is the call number of the book? _____

5. When was the book published? _____

6. What subject might this book be filed under? _____

B. Write author, title, or subject to tell which card you would look for to locate the book or books.

1. books about national parks in the United States _____

2. *The Adventures of Huckleberry Finn* _____

3. a novel by Sylvia Cassidy _____

4. books about Helen Keller _____

5. a book of poems by Vachel Lindsay _____

6. *Children's Verse in America* _____

Using an Encyclopedia

- An **encyclopedia** is a reference book that contains articles on many different subjects. The articles are arranged alphabetically in volumes. Each volume is marked to show which articles are inside.
- Guide words are used to show the first topic on each page.
- At the end of most articles there is a listing of cross-references to related topics for the reader to investigate.

- **Read each sample encyclopedia entry below. Then refer to each to answer the questions that follow.**

> **BIRDSEYE,** Clarence (1886–1956), was an American food expert and inventor. Birdseye was born in Brooklyn, N.Y., and educated at Amherst College. He is best known for developing methods of preserving foods and for marketing quick-frozen foods. He also worked on lighting technology, wood-pulping methods, and heating processes. *See also* FOOD PROCESSING.

1. Whom is the article about? _____

2. When did he live? _____

3. Where did he go to college? _____

4. What is he best known for? _____

5. What else did he work on? _____

6. What other article in the encyclopedia is related to the subject? _____

> **FOOD PROCESSING** is a process by which food is protected from spoiling for future use. Preserved food should look, taste, and feel like the original food. Many methods are used today to preserve food.
> **Canning** In this process, food is sterilized through heat treatments and sealed in airtight containers. Canned food stored in the cold of Antarctica was preserved for 50 years. This would not be true of canned food stored in hot climates.
> **Freezing** The freezing process was not widely used until the late 19th century. Freezing does not kill all types of bacteria, and care must be taken that foods are not thawed and refrozen. Freezing has the advantage of keeping food looking more like the fresh product than canning does.

7. Why do you think this cross-reference is included in the article about Birdseye?

_____

_____

8. Does the above cross-reference mention Clarence Birdseye? _____

Finding an Encyclopedia Article

When looking for an article in the encyclopedia:
- Always look up the last name of a person.
   EXAMPLE: To find an article on Helen Keller, look under <u>Keller</u>.
- Look up the first word in the name of a city, state, or country.
   EXAMPLE: To find an article on Puerto Rico, look under <u>Puerto</u>.
- Look up the most specific word in the name of a geographical location.
   EXAMPLE: To find an article on Lake Erie, look under <u>Erie</u>.
- Look up the most significant word in the name of a general topic.
   EXAMPLE: To find an article on neon lamps, look under <u>neon</u>.

A. The example below shows how the volumes of a particular encyclopedia are marked to indicate the alphabetical range of the articles they cover. Write the number of the volume in which you would find each article.

A	B	C–CH	CI–CZ	D	E	F	G	H	I–J	K	L
1	2	3	4	5	6	7	8	9	10	11	12

M	N	O	P	Q–R	S–SH	SI–SZ	T	U–V	W–X–Y–Z		
13	14	15	16	17	18	19	20	21	22		

1. camping _____

2. North Dakota _____

3. Jonathan Swift _____

4. giant panda _____

5. Nova Scotia _____

6. John F. Kennedy _____

7. Mount Kilimanjaro _____

8. sand flea _____

9. New Guinea _____

10. Babe Ruth _____

11. Caspian Sea _____

12. Smith College _____

13. Victor Hugo _____

14. elementary school _____

15. Lake Ontario _____

B. Look up the following articles in an encyclopedia. Write a cross-reference for each article.

1. bee _____

2. X-ray _____

3. atom _____

4. music _____

5. Georgia _____

6. space travel _____

7. Susan B. Anthony _____

8. cartoon _____

C. Choose a person who interests you, and find the entry for that person in an encyclopedia. Then answer the questions below.

1. Who is the person you've chosen? _____

2. When did this person live? _____

3. What made this person famous? _____

4. What encyclopedia did you use? _____

Lesson 88

Using Visual Aids

- A **chart** lists information in columns, which you read down, and rows, which you read across. The information can be either words or numbers.
- A **graph** can show how quantities change over time. It often shows how two or more things change in relation to one another. The information can be shown through the use of lines, dots, bars, pictures, or in a circle.

A. Use the chart and graph to answer the following questions.

Exercise Chart

Person	Hours Spent Walking	Hours Spent Bicycling
Julia	2	3
Ted	3	3
Miguel	0	6
Kiko	4	2
Terry	3	4

Exercise Graph

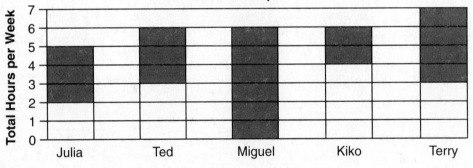

1. Who spent the most time exercising? _____

2. Who spent more time bicycling than walking? _____

3. Who most prefers bicycling to walking? _____

4. Who spent the same amount of time walking as bicycling? _____

5. Is it easier to tell from the chart or the graph who spent the most time exercising?_____

6. Is it easier to tell from the chart or the graph the amount of time spent on each exercise?_____

- A **road map** is another valuable type of visual aid. Maps like the one shown below are helpful when you are unfamiliar with a certain area. To use any map, you should refer to its **legend, compass rose,** and **scale.**
- The legend tells what each symbol on the map represents.
- The compass rose is made up of arrows that point north, south, east, and west.
- The scale allows you to determine how far it is from one location to another. To use the scale, mark the distance between any two locations along the edge of a sheet of paper. Then place the sheet of paper alongside the scale of distance, lining up one of the marks with zero. This will allow you to read the distance between the two locations.

B. Use the map to answer the questions below.

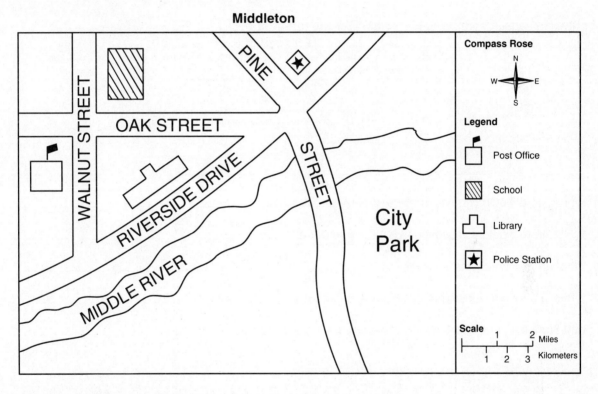

Middleton

1. Is City Park north or south of the river? _____

2. At which intersection is the post office? _____

3. What building is west of the police station? _____

4. Which street is the library on? _____

5. Which street crosses the river? _____

6. What direction is the school from the library? _____

7. What direction does Walnut Street run? _____

8. About how many miles is it from the post office to the police station? _____

Using a Thesaurus

> ■ A **thesaurus** is a reference book that writers use to find the exact words they need. Like a dictionary, a thesaurus lists its entry words alphabetically. Each entry word has a list of **synonyms,** or words that can be used in its place. Some thesauruses also list **antonyms** for the entry word.
>
> EXAMPLE: You have just written the following sentence: The spectators **looked** from the sidelines.
>
> With the help of a thesaurus, you could improve the sentence by replacing looked with its more precise synonym watched.
>
> The spectators **watched** from the sidelines.

A. Use the thesaurus sample below to answer the questions.

> **heat** *n. syn.* warmth, fire, flame, fever, emotion, glow, blush, redness. *ant.* cold, coolness, ice, chilliness

1. Which is the entry word? _____

2. What are its synonyms?_____

_____

3. Which word would you use in place of blaze? _____

4. Which word would you use in place of temperature? _____

5. What are the antonyms of heat? _____

6. Which antonyms would you use in place of hotness? _____

7. What antonym would you use in place of hot? _____

B. Write synonyms of heat to complete the sentences.

1. Eleanor sat by the _____ in the fireplace.

2. Its _____ spread through her body as she relaxed.

3. She felt a warm _____ inside her.

4. Her skin began to show some _____ as she sat there longer.

5. She felt as if she had a _____ .

6. She moved farther away from the flickering _____ .

7. She looked in the mirror and saw the _____ on her face.

8. Happiness was the _____ she felt.

Choosing Reference Sources

- Use a **dictionary** to find the definitions and pronunciations of words, suggestions for word usage, and etymologies.
- Use an **encyclopedia** to find articles about many different people, places, and other subjects. Also use an encyclopedia to find references to related topics.
- Use an **atlas** to find maps and other information about geographical locations.

■ **Write encyclopedia, dictionary, or atlas to show which source you would use to find the following information. Some topics might be found in more than one source.**

1. the pronunciation of the word measure _____

2. the location of Yellowstone National Park _____

3. the care and feeding of a dog _____

4. the distance between Rome and Naples _____

5. jewelry throughout the ages _____

6. planning a vegetable garden _____

7. the meaning of the word federal _____

8. the etymology of the word consider _____

9. the early life of Abraham Lincoln _____

10. the states through which the Mississippi River flows _____

11. how volcanoes form _____

12. a definition of the word ape _____

13. the rivers and mountains of Canada _____

14. how paper is made _____

15. the location of the border between China and the U.S.S.R. _____

16. the history of kite making _____

17. the pronunciation of the word particular _____

18. the names of lakes in Northern California _____

19. the meanings of the homographs of bow _____

20. methods of scoring in football _____

A. Use the dictionary samples to answer the questions below.

tux-e-do (tuk sē′ dō) *n.* a man's formal suit, usually black, having a jacket with satin lapels and trousers with a stripe of satin along the outer side of each leg. [From *Tuxedo* Park, New York, an exclusive community where this suit was popular during the nineteenth century.]

twin (twin) *n.* **1.** one of two offspring born at the same birth. **2.** either of two people, animals, or things that are very much or exactly alike. *-adj.* **1.** being one of two born as twins. **2.** being one of two things that are very much or exactly alike: *The fort had twin towers.* *-v.* to give birth to twins.

1. What part of speech is tuxedo? _____

2. How many definitions are given for tuxedo? _____

3. How many definitions are given for the noun twin? _____

4. Which word can be used as an adjective? _____

5. Which word comes from the name of a place in New York? _____

6. How many syllables are there in tuxedo? _____

   in twin? _____

7. What parts of speech is twin? _____

8. Underline the pair of words that could be guide words for the dictionary entries above.

   a. turtle / twill   **c.** tusk / twirl

   b. twang / twist   **d.** Tuscan / twig

B. Write the part of the book you would use to answer the following questions.

1. What is the name of Chapter 2? _____

2. Who wrote the book? _____

3. When was the book published? _____

4. Does the book have information on Martin Luther King, Jr.? _____

C. Write the answers to the questions below.

1. How are books arranged on library shelves? _____

2. What are the three types of cards each book has in a card catalog? _____

3. Which type of card would you use to locate a book by Ansel Adams? _____

D. On the first line, write the word you would look under in an encyclopedia to find an article on the topic. On the second line, write a possible cross-reference.

1. New Zealand _____ _____

2. South Carolina _____ _____

3. palm trees _____ _____

E. Use the map to answer the questions.

City Park

1. What direction is the lake from the camping area? _____

2. How far is parking from the camping area? _____

3. Which direction would you go to get to the camping area from the showers? _____

F. Use the thesaurus sample below to answer the questions.

> **sweet** *adj.* **syn.** pleasant, pure, fresh, sugary. **ant.** sour, acid, unripe, harsh

1. What is the entry word? _____

2. What are its synonyms? _____

3. Which word would you use in place of charming? _____

G. Write encyclopedia, dictionary, or atlas to show which source you would use to find the following information.

1. the definition of the word realistic _____

2. the location of the Gulf of Mexico _____

3. the history of the Civil War _____

A. Find the word fallacy in the dictionary. Then answer the questions.

1. Write the guide words from the page on which you found the entry for fallacy. _____

2. Write the word fallacy in syllables. _____

3. What part of speech is the word fallacy? _____

4. Write a sentence using the word fallacy. _____

5. Write two ways in which fallacy may be divided at the end of a writing line. _____

6. Write the respelling of fallacy. _____

B. Use a textbook with an index to answer the questions.

1. Copy the title from the title page. _____

2. Write the name(s) of the author(s). _____

3. What is the name of the publisher? _____

4. Name two other pieces of information that you can find on the copyright page. _____

_____

C. Use the sample catalog card to answer the questions.

```
            RAIN FOREST
574.5
M235     Macdonald, Fiona
              New view: Rain forest–
         Austin, TX: Raintree/Steck-Vaughn, ©1994
              32 p.: col. illus.
```

1. What kind of catalog card is this? _____

   a. title card   **b.** subject card   **c.** author card

2. Who is the author of this book? _____

3. What is the title? _____

4. Who is the publisher? _____

5. Is the book illustrated? _____

6. What is the call number? _____

D. Use an encyclopedia to complete the following exercises.

1. What is the name of the encyclopedia you are using?

   _____

2. List the volume number in which you would find each topic in your encyclopedia.

   _____ **a.** New Orleans   _____ **h.** Puerto Rico

   _____ **b.** North Carolina   _____ **i.** post office

   _____ **c.** Mount Holly   _____ **j.** Benjamin Franklin

   _____ **d.** Niagara Falls   _____ **k.** country music

   _____ **e.** Mahatma Gandhi   _____ **l.** Thames River

   _____ **f.** New Zealand   _____ **m.** Indian Ocean

   _____ **g.** Olympic Games   _____ **n.** Walt Disney

3. Look up each subject in your encyclopedia. Write a cross-reference for each subject.

   a. appaloosa _____

   b. Lincoln Memorial _____

   c. canoe racing _____

   d. pirate _____

   e. library _____

   f. Robert R. Livingston _____

E. Use the information in the chart to complete the bar graph. Then answer the questions below.

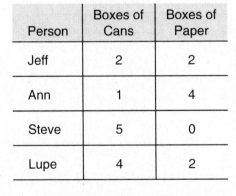

Recycling Chart

Person	Boxes of Cans	Boxes of Paper
Jeff	2	2
Ann	1	4
Steve	5	0
Lupe	4	2

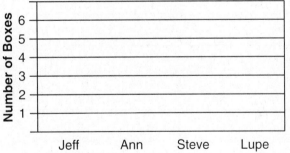

Recycling Graph

Number of Boxes: 6 5 4 3 2 1

Jeff   Ann   Steve   Lupe

Graph Key

Cans

Paper

1. Which two people recycled the same amount of paper? _____

2. Who recycled the most cans? _____

3. Who recycled the most materials altogether? _____

4. Is it easier to tell from the chart or the graph who recycled the most of each material? _____

Synonyms and Antonyms ■ On the line before each pair of words, write S if they are synonyms or A if they are antonyms.

1. _____ far, close

2. _____ discover, find

3. _____ shut, close

4. _____ mistake, error

5. _____ jagged, smooth

6. _____ yell, shout

7. _____ tall, short

8. _____ easy, simple

9. _____ together, apart

10. _____ honest, truthful

11. _____ clean, dirty

12. _____ tired, rested

13. _____ join, unite

14. _____ burn, scorch

15. _____ hit, strike

Homonyms ■ Underline the correct homonym in each sentence below.

1. He drove the wooden (steaks, stakes) into the ground.

2. We will (meet, meat) at Rosa's house tonight.

3. The audience thought the dull speaker was a (boar, bore).

4. The team (needs, kneads) more practice.

5. Homemade (bred, bread) smells wonderful when it is baking.

6. His (sun, son) plays on a professional basketball team.

7. The (plane, plain) couldn't take off in the heavy fog.

8. We (heard, herd) a strange noise outside the cabin.

Homographs ■ Write sentences for each of the homographs below. Use a different meaning in each sentence.

1. (set) _____

(set) _____

2. (rose) _____

(rose) _____

3. (fan) _____

(fan) _____

4. (live) _____

(live) _____

5. (tear) _____

(tear) _____

Prefixes and Suffixes ■ Add a prefix or suffix to the underlined word in each sentence to form a new word that makes sense in the sentence. Write the new word in the blank.

1. I've always said that anything is <u>possible</u> if you always tell yourself that nothing is _____ .

2. That man's business is a <u>success</u>, and he thanks his employees for making the past year the most

   _____ in the company's history.

3. It took many hours to <u>write</u> and then _____ the term paper to get it ready to hand in.

4. None of us were <u>certain</u> why we felt so _____ about which road to take.

Contractions and Compound Words ■ Write the two words that make up the contraction in each sentence. Then underline the compound word in each sentence, and draw a line between the two words that make up each compound word.

1. _____ _____ "Where's the airplane museum?" asked Anne.

2. _____ _____ "I think it's downtown," said Steve.

3. _____ _____ "Isn't that the headquarters of the parachute club?" asked Tim.

4. _____ _____ "Yes, they're in the same high-rise," said Steve.

Connotation ■ Use the connotation of each underlined word below to answer the questions.

1. Which is more unattractive, a <u>plain</u> jacket or a <u>homely</u> jacket? _____

2. Would an <u>old</u> house or a <u>deteriorated</u> house probably be the better buy? _____

3. Did the critic like the movie more if he <u>raved</u> about it or <u>talked</u> about it? _____

4. Would a <u>fascinating</u> speaker or an <u>interesting</u> speaker be more enjoyable? _____

Idioms ■ Underline the idiom in each sentence. On the line after each sentence, explain what the idiom means. Use a dictionary if necessary.

1. We hit the sack early after our exhausting trip.

   _____

2. We were left high and dry on the island when our boat sank.

   _____

3. Our plans for the surprise party are up in the air.

   _____

4. I'm all thumbs when I try to build anything.

   _____

Types of Sentences ■ Before each sentence, write **D** for declarative, **IN** for interrogative, **IM** for imperative, **E** for exclamatory, or **X** if it is not a sentence. Punctuate each sentence correctly.

1. _____ I can't believe that fish got away ____

2. _____ Where do you think it went ____

3. _____ Under those rocks over there ____

4. _____ Have you ever lost a fish ____

5. _____ Many, many times ____

6. _____ I always throw the small fish back ____

7. _____ Toss your line in over here ____

8. _____ Where's the best spot ____

9. _____ Near those trees in the middle ____

10. _____ I feel lucky ____

11. _____ Look at that splash ____

12. _____ I think it's a trout ____

Subjects and Predicates ■ Draw a line between the complete subject and the complete predicate in each sentence below. Underline the simple subject once and the simple predicate twice. Circle the sentence that is in inverted order.

1. Bicycling is a sport that people of all ages can enjoy.

2. Cyclists can learn hand signals and traffic rules.

3. Many cyclists wear special biking clothes and shoes.

4. A helmet is an important safety item.

5. Experts recommend that cyclists always ride with the flow of traffic.

6. City riders should learn how to ride in traffic.

7. All people who ride bicycles should obey the traffic laws.

8. Are you a careful and considerate cyclist?

Compound Subjects and Predicates ■ In each sentence below, draw a line between the complete subject and the complete predicate. Then write **CS** if the subject is compound or **CP** if the predicate is compound.

_____ 1. John Scott is concerned about car pollution and rides his bicycle to work.

_____ 2. His wife and two children ride their bicycles to work and to school, too.

_____ 3. John and his wife run errands on their bicycles whenever possible.

_____ 4. The Scott children visit friends and go to after-school activities on their bicycles.

_____ 5. The Scott family helps save the environment and gets plenty of exercise.

_____ 6. Victoria and Nick Scott think that bicycling is good for them and good for the earth.

Compound Sentences ■ **Combine each pair of sentences below to form a compound sentence.**

1. A bicycle safety course is offered at our neighborhood center. The class is for children and adults together.

_____

_____

2. People are taught important traffic rules. They learn ways to prevent bicycle thefts.

_____

_____

3. Everyone must pass a final bicycling test. They will not get a certificate if they fail.

_____

_____

Correcting Run-on Sentences and Expanding Sentences ■ **Correct the run-on sentences. Then expand each new sentence by adding details.**

1. The cyclists rode, the rider in front led.

   a. _____

   b. _____

2. Two cyclists sped up, they pursued the leader.

   a. _____

   b. _____

3. A bicycle chain broke the leader fell behind.

   a. _____

   b. _____

4. Judges held stopwatches, riders crossed the finish line.

   a. _____

   b. _____

5. The race was over the spectators cheered.

   a. _____

   b. _____

Parts of Speech ■ Write the part of speech above each underlined word. Use the abbreviations in the box.

n. noun	adj. adjective	pp. prepositional phrase
int. interjection	adv. adverb	conj. conjunction
v. verb	prep. preposition	pron. pronoun

1. Mary swam in the lake until dark.

2. The fussy baby finally went to sleep.

3. Wow! That marble statue is really beautiful!

4. Nora and I worked late at the office.

5. Citizens of the democratic countries exercise their right to vote in elections.

6. Pets are a source of companionship for many people.

7. She became the busiest supervisor at Hart Industries.

8. Recycling programs to protect our environment have become popular in most cities.

Verbs ■ Underline the correct verb to complete each sentence.

1. You (was, were) the first person hired.

2. She (will complete, completed) her driving course last week.

3. We have (saw, seen) all of her movies.

4. My friend (came, come) by train to visit me.

5. She hasn't (did, done) any preparation for her speech.

6. Who (drank, drunk) the last soda?

7. The volunteers haven't (ate, eaten) since breakfast.

8. We (rang, rung) the alarm at the first sign of danger.

9. Maria has (sang, sung) the national anthem at every game.

10. Have you (chose, chosen) your wedding dress yet?

11. The stereo was (broke, broken) when we bought it.

12. The passengers (grew, grown) tired of all the delays.

13. Sara has (went, gone) back to college.

14. Has Mr. Hall (gave, given) you the tickets yet?

15. Kara has (wrote, written) in her journal every day for a year.

Trees are important for _____ products and their benefits to the
(possessive pronoun)

environment. Wood _____ one of the main building supplies in the
(present tense of <u>be</u>)

world and an important fuel. Paper and paper products _____ from
(helping verb and verb)

wood pulp. Trees also _____ _____ nuts
(present tense verb)   (adjective)

and fruits for both _____ and humans.
(common noun)

One way _____ help the environment is by releasing oxygen
(plural of <u>tree</u>)

_____ the air. For instance, if a tree has _____
(preposition)   (past participle of <u>take</u>)

in sunlight and carbon dioxide, it _____ oxygen. Tree roots help
(future tense of <u>release</u>)

control erosion and flooding. Trees have always _____ homes
(past participle of <u>give</u>)

_____ shelter for _____ animals.
(conjunction)   (adjective)

Raccoons, _____, and other animals _____
(common noun)   (present tense verb)

their homes _____ trees.
(preposition)

_____ trees have lived and _____ for
(adjective)   (past participle of <u>grow</u>)

thousands of years and are hundreds of feet tall. The redwoods in California are some of the

_____ trees in the world. The tallest tree is 364 feet tall and lives
(superlative adjective)

_____ Humboldt National Forest. The _____
(preposition)   (superlative adjective)

living tree is a bristlecone pine in the state of Nevada that is _____
(adverb)

4,600 years old.

Capitalization and End Punctuation ▪ Circle each letter that should be capitalized.
Write the capital letter above it. Add correct end punctuation to each sentence.

1. "how do you feel about cable television ____" asked marie.

2. her friends looked at her in surprise ____

3. "it's wonderful ____" said peter.

4. marie looked at peter and george ____

5. "i like it," said george, "but it costs too much to get everything ____"

6. "i'd like to have the movie channels," marie said ____

7. "then why don't you just get one of them ____" asked peter.

8. marie didn't know that she could request only one channel ____

9. "that's a great idea ____" she exclaimed.

10. peter and george had helped marie solve her problem ____

Punctuation and Capitalization ▪ Circle each letter that should be capitalized below.
Add commas, quotation marks, apostrophes, periods, colons, and hyphens where needed.

122 e. park street
denver, co 81442
october 10, 1994

mr. marshall chase
3910 prairie avenue
lowell, ma 01740

Dear mr. chase

thank you very much for your interest in my star gazing book a guide to the stars____ i published it in september through a well known astronomy publisher the skys the limit press____ according to my publisher, books will be available at bookstores this month____

i have the answer to your question on how I do my research____ i have a very powerful telescope that i use every day____ i do most of my work at night between 1015 P.M. and 130 A.M. i find those to be the darkest hours out here in colorado____ finally, i have a piece of advice for budding astronomers____ always keep a journal of the stars you see each night and try to memorize their location____ i always say to my students the skys the limit____ good luck star gazing____

Sincerely,
professor liz nelson

Commas and Quotation Marks ■ In the following example of a news conference, add commas and quotation marks where needed.

Ted Carter a United Nations spokesperson announced Many remote towns and villages in Mexico have been destroyed by a major earthquake and the United States and Canada are sending emergency relief. International troops will help with fires flooding and injuries resulting from the earthquake. The spokesperson further stated Colonel Marks commander of relief troops will oversee medical staff rescue crews and cleanup operations. Mr. Carter said The troops will provide medical supplies food water and temporary shelter for the earthquake victims. He ended his statement by saying The troops are preparing now and they should begin arriving in Mexico tomorrow morning. Mr. Carter then told the reporters that he would answer some questions.

Mr. Carter are any more countries involved in the relief efforts? asked Dorian Kramer reporter for the *Richland Register.*

Mr. Carter replied Yes. England France and Germany are also sending supplies and medical staff.

Pete Simmons KRSS reporter asked How long will our troops be in Mexico?

Mr. Carter responded Well the President is not sure but we expect the troops to be there several weeks.

Joe Kelly *Up-Date* magazine reporter asked How many deaths and injuries have been reported?

We do not have exact figures but we know there are many people hurt and missing said Mr. Carter.

Apostrophes, Colons, and Hyphens ■ Add apostrophes, colons, and hyphens where needed in the sentences.

1. The boys father didn't want them to stay home alone.
2. Of all the countries Ive visited, these countries scenery impressed me most England, France, and Switzerland.
3. The flowers petals werent as colorful as the pictures showed them to be.
4. The Los Angeles mayors speeches at the national mayors convention will be at these times 500 P.M., 730 P.M., and 900 P.M.
5. My houses roof wasnt damaged by hail, but other houses roofs were Jims roof, my father in laws roof, my cousins roof, and Ms. Browns roof.
6. Many children attend our public librarys childrens hour on Tuesdays from 900 A.M. to 1000 A.M.
7. The new stores advertisement said it specializes in mens and womens clothing, ladies jewelry, and perfumes from around the world.
8. The winners trophy will be awarded to one of the twenty two contestants.

Topic Sentences ■ Write a topic sentence for the paragraphs below. Name a possible audience for each paragraph.

1.   All children and adults should learn basic first aid. Courses are offered through schools and community groups. You never know when you'll need to clean a wound or use a more difficult technique during an emergency. By knowing first aid, you'll always be prepared.

Topic Sentence: _____

Audience: _____

2.   Butterflies and moths fly from flower to flower, looking for pollen. When they land on a flower, some of the sticky pollen rubs off on their legs. When they fly to another flower, it rubs off onto the new flower.

Topic Sentence: _____

Audience: _____

3.   Many people walk or run to stay healthy. Others swim or play sports for exercise. Some people prefer indoor exercises, such as using exercise videos and machines.

Topic Sentence: _____

Audience: _____

Supporting Details ■ Underline the two sentences that contain details that support the topic sentence.

1. **Topic Sentence:** A meteor looks like a bright streak of light in the sky.

   a. A meteor leaves a trail of hot gas.

   b. A meteor blazes across the sky as it travels through space.

   c. I saw a meteor fall from the sky.

2. **Topic Sentence:** Ants are called social insects.

   a. Ants live together in colonies and help each other.

   b. Ants are pests, and they can ruin a picnic.

   c. Ants share their food and their work.

3. **Topic Sentence:** Alligators and crocodiles are alike in many ways.

   a. Alligators have wider heads and shorter jaws than crocodiles.

   b. They are both reptiles and have rough skin.

   c. Alligators and crocodiles live in and near the water.

Revising and Proofreading ▪ Rewrite the paragraphs below. Correct the errors by following the proofreader's marks.

Proofreader's Marks

≡
Capitalize.

⊙
Add a period.

⑤ⓟ
Correct spelling.

/
Make a small letter.

∧
Add something.

¶
Indent for new paragraph.

∧
Add a comma.

ℯ
Take something out.

⟶
Move something.

¶ did you know that roughly three-quarters of the earth's fresh water is held not in rivers and lakes?

the water is held in glaciers, lage sheets of ice that form in high altitudes and polar regions such

as antarctica and Greenland their are between 70,000 and 200,000 glaicers in the world.

¶ as temperatures warm, glaciers melt a little and move at a wrate that can't bee seen, as they

move, they sometimes freize and add to their mass before moving on they actually reshape

The land they pass ovver the most famus glaciers are in europe the best-known ones are

in the french and swiss alps.

Using the Dictionary ▪ Use the dictionary samples to answer the questions.

firm (furm) *adj.* **1.** unyielding to pressure; steady **2.** unchanging, established. *The company had a firm customer base.* **3.** tough and hard. *The apple had a firm skin.* *-n.* a business partnership. [Old French *ferme*, meaning strong]

fleet (flēt) *n.* **1.** a group of battle or warships under unified command. **2.** a group operating or working (such as ships, cars, or planes) under unified command. *The fleet of trucks reported to their dispatcher at 5:00 A.M.* [Old English *fleot*, meaning a ship or ships.]

1. Circle the letter of the guide words for the above entries.

　　a. flag / fleece　　　**b.** float / flood　　　**c.** fire / flight

2. How many definitions are listed for firm? _____ fleet? _____

3. What part of speech is fleet? _____

4. How many syllables do fleet and firm have? _____

5. Write the respelling of fleet. _____ firm. _____

6. Which word came from the Old French word ferme? _____

Parts of a Book ▪ Write title page, table of contents, index, or copyright page to tell where each of the following would be found.

1. the page on which Lesson 12 begins _____

2. information about the Revolutionary War _____

3. where the book was published _____

4. the author of the book _____

Reference Sources ▪ Write encyclopedia, dictionary, thesaurus, or atlas to tell where you would find the following information.

1. the height of Mt. Everest _____

2. the definition of the word astronomy _____

3. the birthdate of George Washington _____

4. an antonym for the word yell _____

5. the location of the border between Canada and the United States _____

6. how earthquakes develop _____

7. a synonym for the word carry _____

8. the etymology of the word pencil _____

Using the Library and the Card Catalog ■ **Use the sample catalog card to answer the questions.**

```
302.2
S28     Sauvain, Philip Arthur.
        Breakthrough: Communications—
        Austin: Raintree/Steck-Vaughn, © 1990.
        48 p.
```

1. Who is the author? _____

2. What is the book's call number? _____

3. When was the book published? _____

4. Who is the publisher? _____

Using Visual Aids ■ **Use the information in the chart to complete the graph. Then answer the questions below.**

Fishing Chart

Day	Number of Cod	Number of Tuna
Monday	15	10
Tuesday	20	15
Wednesday	10	20
Thursday	5	30
Friday	15	15

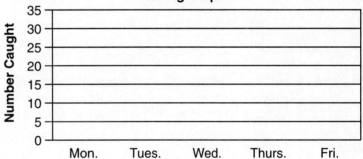

Fishing Graph

1. On which days were 35 total fish caught? _____

2. On which day were equal amounts of cod and tuna caught? _____

3. On which day was twice as much tuna as cod caught? _____

4. Is it easier to tell from the graph or the chart which days were the best for fishing? _____

A. Write **S** before each pair of synonyms, **A** before each pair of antonyms, and **H** before each pair of homonyms.

_____ **1.** it's, its   _____ **3.** heavy, light

_____ **2.** bright, shiny   _____ **4.** vain, vane

B. Write the homograph for the pair of meanings.

_____ **a.** clever, intelligent   **b.** a sharp, stinging pain

C. Write **P** before each word with a prefix, **S** before each word with a suffix, and **C** before each compound word.

_____ **1.** newspaper   _____ **3.** nonsense

_____ **2.** reasonable   _____ **4.** doubtful

D. Write the words that make up each contraction.

_____ **1.** they've   _____ **2.** we'd

E. Underline the word in parentheses that has the more positive connotation.

Her (clever, sneaky) actions helped her win the prize.

F. Circle the letter of the idiom that means **strange** or **unusual**.

a. off the wall   **b.** crazy like a fox

G. Write **D** before the declarative sentence, **IM** before the imperative sentence, **E** before the exclamatory sentence, and **IN** before the interrogative sentence. Then circle the simple subject, and underline the simple predicate in each sentence.

_____ **1.** Make up your mind.   _____ **3.** That really hurts!

_____ **2.** How are you feeling?   _____ **4.** I will be there soon.

H. Write **CS** before the sentence that has a compound subject. Write **CP** before the sentence that has a compound predicate.

_____ **1.** Carl and Juanita went to the movies.

_____ **2.** The audience clapped and cheered.

I. Write **CS** before the compound sentence. Write **RO** before the run-on sentence. Write **I** before the sentence that is in inverted order.

_____ **1.** Off came the cold, wet jacket.

_____ **2.** Her mother was born in Rome, and her father was born in Venice.

_____ **3.** He went faster than he should have, he wrecked his car.

J. Underline the common nouns in the sentence. Circle the proper nouns in the sentence.

The newspaper told about the departure of Juan Carlos from the country of Chile.

K. Write the correct possessive noun to complete the second sentence.

The glasses of Maria were scratched. _____ glasses were scratched.

L. Underline the appositive in the sentence. Circle the noun it identifies or explains.

It was the new visitor, Kevin, who had the most interesting ideas.

M. Underline the verb phrase, and circle the helping verb.

He is still having doubts about his dinner party.

N. Write past, present, or future to show the tense of each underlined verb.

_____ **1.** In a few minutes, that new show will come on.

_____ **2.** I watched the funniest movie last night.

_____ **3.** Try to take your time.

O. Circle the correct verbs in each sentence.

1. They tried to (drink, drank) the lemonade, but it was (froze, frozen).

2. The plane (went, gone) to Boston before it (fly, flew) to Quebec.

3. The child (broke, broken) the window when he (threw, throw) the ball toward the house.

P. Write SP before the sentence that has a subject pronoun, OP before the sentence that has an object pronoun, PP before the sentence that has a possessive pronoun, and IP before the sentence that has an indefinite pronoun. Circle the pronoun in each sentence.

_____ **1.** Everyone saw something different. _____ **3.** The spot in the sky looked like a balloon to her.

_____ **2.** He said the object was an airplane. _____ **4.** Their opposite opinions caused an argument.

Q. On the line before each sentence, write adjective or adverb to describe the underlined word.

_____ **1.** You seem very happy.

_____ **2.** She spoke slowly and clearly.

_____ **3.** The German book was interesting.

_____ **4.** He is the friendliest person I know.

R. Circle the correct word in each sentence.

1. You (may, can) use my pen to take notes.

2. Please (sit, set) on the sofa and rest.

3. I will (learn, teach) you how to cook.

4. He has (layed, lain) down to rest.

5. It (don't, doesn't) make any sense to me.

S. Underline each prepositional phrase twice. Circle each preposition. Underline the conjunction once.

I think we will find the solution to the problem, and everyone will agree on it.

T. Rewrite the letter. Use capital letters and punctuation marks where needed.

733 w martin

paducah ky 55809

mar 13 1994

dear ms simpson

please send me twenty one copies of the pamphlet dont ever stop trying _____ my students will enjoy its positive message _____ ive enclosed an addressed and stamped envelope for your convenience _____ thank you _____

yours truly

leslie stone

_____

_____

_____

_____

_____

_____

_____

_____

_____

_____

U. Write a topic sentence and two sentences with descriptive supporting details on the topic of finding a job.

_____

_____

_____

V. Number the steps for writing a report in order.

_____ **1.** Organize your research questions.   _____ **4.** Make an outline.

_____ **2.** Look in an encyclopedia.   _____ **5.** Write information in your own words.

_____ **3.** Write the report.   _____ **6.** Revise and proofread your report.

W. Circle the part that does not belong in a business letter.

closing   outline   heading   signature   body   greeting

X. Use the dictionary entry below to answer the questions.

harvest (här' vist) *n.* **1.** the act of gathering a crop: *The harvest was successful.* **2.** the result of an action: *Her words brought a harvest of complaints.*

1. What part of speech is the word harvest? _____

2. Would hatch come before or after harvest in the dictionary? _____

3. Would harp / hate or have / hay be the guide words for harvest? _____

4. Write the number of the definition for harvest in this sentence: Our favorite time is during harvest. _____

5. Write the word for this respelling: (kəm plānt'). _____

6. Write harvest separated into syllables. _____

Y. Circle the information found in the table of contents of a book.

the publisher's name   where a chapter begins   where specific information is found

Z. Write the source from the box that you would use to find the information listed.

| dictionary   card catalog   encyclopedia   atlas |

_____ **1.** books on a specific subject

_____ **2.** the origin of a word

_____ **3.** the location of a country

_____ **4.** an article on James Monroe

_____ **5.** the distance from Montreal to Boston

Below is a list of the sections on *Check What You've Learned* and the pages on which the skills in each section are taught. If you missed any questions, turn to the pages listed and practice the skills. Then correct the problems you missed on *Check What You've Learned*.

Section	Practice Page	Section	Practice Page	Section	Practice Page
Unit 1		*Unit 3*		*Unit 4*	
A	5, 6	J	33–35	T	86–94
B	7	K	38, 39		
C	8, 9, 11	L	40	*Unit 5*	
D	10	M	41–44	U	100–102
E	12	N	46	V	103–107
F	13	O	48–55	W	108, 109
Unit 2		P	56–63	*Unit 6*	
G	19, 20, 22	Q	64–73	X	114–117
H	24, 25	R	74–76	Y	119
I	23, 26, 27	S	77–79	Z	120–127

Check What You Know (P. 1)

A. 1. A
2. H
3. S
4. H

B. can

C. 1. S
2. C
3. P
4. P

D. 1. can not
2. they will

E. curious

F. b

G. The words in bold should be circled.
1. IN, **Who**, is going
2. E, **I**, feel
3. IM, **(You)**, do worry
4. D, **It**, is

H. 1. CP
2. CS

I. 1. RO
2. I
3. CS

J. The words in bold should be circled.
The police officer told **Paul** that **Judge Hawkins** was the person who would decide.

Check What You Know (P. 2)

K. friend's

L. The words in bold should be circled.

Nolan Ryan, a baseball star, is signing autographs at the store.

M. The word in bold should be circled.

He **will** soon discover the error in his plan.

N. 1. past
2. future
3. present

O. 1. flew, went
2. drank, threw
3. froze, broke

P. The words in bold should be circled.

1. SP, **You**   3. PP, **her**
2. IP, **Nobody**   4. OP, **us**

Q. 1. adjective   3. adverb
2. adverb   4. adjective

R. 1. Can   4. laid
2. learn   5. doesn't
3. set

S. The words in bold should be circled.
You can either wait **in** the car or **outside** the door.

Check What You Know (P. 3)

T.   832 Southern Star
Helena, MT 95097
Aug. 27, 1994

Dear Edward,
I have the information you wanted. Did you ever think I'd get it to you this quickly? Well, it's time I surprised you. Here's what you should bring: six cartons of orange juice, forty-five paper cups, and three bags of ice. What a breakfast party this will be!

Your friend,
Bill

U. Discuss your answers with your instructor.

V. 1. 5   4. 2
2. 1   5. 3
3. 6   6. 4

W. title

Check What You Know (P. 4)

X. 1. noun   4. 2
2. after   5. surface
3. care / carrot   6. car-pet

Y. the author's name

Z. 1. atlas or encyclopedia   4. card catalog
2. encyclopedia   5. encyclopedia
3. dictionary

Unit 1 Vocabulary

Lesson 1, Synonyms and Antonyms (P. 5)

A. Discuss your answers with your instructor.

B. 1. begin   4. tired
2. fall   5. close
3. sick

C. Discuss your answers with your instructor.

D. 1. heavy   4. empty
2. late   5. found
3. kind

Lesson 2, Homonyms (P. 6)

A. 1. beach
2. deer
3. weigh
4. pane
5. to, to, two
6. knew, new
7. their
8. ate, eight
9. sea
10. Ring
11. here
12. write, right
13. read
14. buy, by
15. tale

B. 1. haul
2. through
3. week
4. they're or their
5. herd
6. hear
7. buy or bye
8. pain
9. heel or he'll
10. blue
11. flour
12. stare
13. pail
14. wring
15. sore
16. sail
17. one
18. I'll or isle
19. road or rowed
20. meat or mete
21. hour
22. see
23. write or rite
24. piece
25. know
26. great
27. weigh or whey
28. sent or scent
29. do or due
30. fourth

Lesson 3, Homographs (P. 7)

A. 1. checks
2. interest
3. vault
4. interest
5. vault
6. checks

B. Discuss your answers with your instructor.

1. a
2. a
3. a
4. a
5. b

Lesson 4, Prefixes (P. 8)

A. Discuss your answers with your instructor.

1. impractical
2. misbehave
3. uneasy
4. nonviolent
5. unusual

B. Discuss your answers with your instructor.

1. un-
2. dis-
3. dis-
4. mis-
5. pre-
6. re-
7. mis-
8. im-
9. non-
10. un-
11. in-
12. pre-

Lesson 5, Suffixes (P. 9)

A. Discuss your answers with your instructor.

1. mountainous
2. helpful
3. snowy
4. national
5. knowledgeable

B. Discuss your answers with your instructor.

1. -able
2. -less
3. -ous
4. -able
5. -ous
6. -able
7. -ous
8. -ful
9. -y
10. -less
11. -al
12. -al

Lesson 6, Contractions (P. 10)

A. 1. they're, they are
2. won't, will not
3. There's, There is
4. That's, That is; shouldn't, should not
5. weren't, were not
6. doesn't, does not
7. can't, cannot; it's, it is
8. they've, they have; they'll, they will
9. It's, It is; aren't, are not
10. they'd, they would

B. 1. I have, I've; I would, I'd
2. It is, It's; what is, what's
3. I will, I'll
4. does not, doesn't

Lesson 7, Compound Words (P. 11)

A. Discuss your answers with your instructor.

B. 1. forehead
2. haircut
3. everywhere
4. newsstand
5. loudspeaker
6. everything

Lesson 8, Connotation/Denotation (P. 12)

A. 1. wonderful
2. Brave
3. fascinating
4. hilarious
5. smile

B. 1. cheap
2. soggy
3. nagged
4. silly
5. smirk
6. frightened

C. 1. antique
2. slender
3. thrifty
4. parade
5. disaster
6. sip
7. starving
8. filthy

Lesson 9, Idioms (P. 13)

A. 1. j
2. i
3. h
4. a
5. e
6. f
7. d
8. g
9. b
10. c

B. Discuss your answers with your instructor.

1. in hot water
2. beside themselves
3. fly off the handle
4. shaken up
5. talk turkey

Review (P. 14)

A. Discuss your answers with your instructor.

B. 1. plane, there   3. bear, would
2. week, to, see   4. cheap, break, week

C. Discuss your answers with your instructor.

  1. a   3. a
  2. b   4. b

D. Discuss your answers with your instructor.

  1. im-, not possible
  2. in-, not complete
  3. un-, not easy
  4. non-, not violent
  5. dis-, not interested
  6. re-, furnish again
  7. mis-, pronounce incorrectly
  8. pre-, before history

Review (P. 15)

E. 1. -ous, full of hazards
  2. -less, without help
  3. -able, to be able to profit
  4. -al, relating to a region

F. 1. we'll   4. they've
2. she'd   5. you'll
3. won't   6. we're

G. 1. crossroad   3. snowplow
2. sandlot   4. tabletop

H. 1. inexpensive   3. curious
2. cozy   4. relaxed

I. Discuss your answers with your instructor.

  1. stay on your toes   3. saw red
  2. run across   4. all ears

Using What You've Learned (P. 16)

A. Discuss your answers with your instructor.

B. Discuss your answers with your instructor.

C. Discuss your answers with your instructor.

  1. knew   4. wait
  2. greater   5. waste
  3. chews

D. Discuss your answers with your instructor.

Using What You've Learned (P. 17)

E. Discuss your answers with your instructor.

F. Discuss your answers with your instructor.

G. Words may vary. Suggested:

  1. soggy; moist   6. rags; apparel
  2. holler; call   7. beg; request
  3. skinny; slender   8. chore; job
  4. ancient; elderly   9. hack; carve
  5. gab; discuss   10. devour; dine

Unit 2   Sentences

Lesson 10, Recognizing Sentences (P. 18)

S should precede the following sentences, and each should end with a period: 2, 5, 7, 9, 10, 11, 12, 13, 16, 19, 20, 21, 22, 24, 28, 29.

Lesson 11, Types of Sentences (P. 19)

1. IN		15. IN
2. IN		16. D
3. D		17. D
4. D		18. IN
5. D		19. D
6. IN		20. IN
7. D		21. IN
8. D		22. D
9. IN		23. D
10. IN		24. IN
11. D		25. D
12. D		26. IN
13. IN		27. IN
14. D		28. D

Lesson 12, More Types of Sentences (P. 20)

1. IM		15. E
2. IM		16. E
3. E		17. E
4. IM		18. IM
5. E		19. IM
6. IM or E		20. E
7. IM		21. E
8. IM		22. IM
9. IM		23. E
10. IM		24. IM
11. E		25. IM
12. IM		26. IM
13. E		27. E
14. E		28. E

Lesson 13, Complete Subjects and Predicates (P. 21)

  1. Bees / fly.
  2. Trains / whistle.
  3. A talented artist / drew . . .
  4. The wind / blew . . .
  5. My grandmother / made . . .
  6. We / surely . . .

7. These cookies / are . . .
8. This letter / came . . .
9. They / rent . . .
10. Jennifer / is . . .
11. Our baseball team / won . . .
12. The band / played . . .
13. A cloudless sky / is . . .
14. The voice of the auctioneer / was . . .
15. A sudden flash of lightning / startled . . .
16. The wind / howled . . .
17. Paul's dog / followed . . .
18. Their apartment / is . . .
19. We / have . . .
20. Each player on the team / deserves . . .
21. Forest rangers / fought . . .
22. A friend / taught . . .
23. Millions of stars / make . . .
24. The airplane / was . . .
25. Many of the children / waded . . .
26. Yellowstone Park / is . . .
27. Cold weather / is . . .
28. The trees / were . . .

Lesson 14, Simple Subjects and Predicates (P. 22)

1. A sudden clap of thunder / frightened . . .
2. The soft snow / covered . . .
3. We / drove . . .
4. The students / are making . . .
5. Our class / read . . .
6. The women / were talking . . .
7. This album / has . . .
8. We / are furnishing . . .
9. All the trees on that lawn / are . . .
10. Many Americans / are working . . .
11. The manager / read . . .
12. Bill / brought . . .
13. We / opened . . .
14. The two mechanics / worked . . .
15. Black and yellow butterflies / fluttered . . .
16. The child / spoke . . .
17. We / found . . .
18. The best part of the program / is . . .
19. Every ambitious person / is working . . .
20. Sheryl / swam . . .
21. Our program / will begin . . .
22. The handle of this basket / is broken.
23. The clock in the tower / strikes . . .
24. The white farmhouse on that road / belongs . . .
25. The first game of the season / will be played . . .

Lesson 15, Subjects and Predicates in Inverted Order (P. 23)

A. Sentences 1, 3, 4, 5, 6, 8, 9, 11, and 12 are in inverted order.

1. Lightly falls / the mist.
2. The peaches on this tree / are ripe now.
3. Over and over rolled / the rocks.
4. Down the street marched / the band.
5. Near the ocean are / many birds.
6. Right under the chair ran / the kitten.
7. He / hit the ball a long way.
8. Along the ridge hiked / the campers.
9. Underground is / the stream.
10. The fish / jumped in the lake.
11. Over the hill came / the trucks.
12. Out came / the rainbow.

B. 1. The mist falls lightly.
   2. The rocks rolled over and over.
   3. The band marched down the street.
   4. Many birds are near the ocean.
   5. The kitten ran right under the chair.
   6. The campers hiked along the ridge.
   7. The stream is underground.
   8. The rainbow came out.

Lesson 16, Using Compound Subjects (P. 24)

A. Sentences 1, 2, 3, 4, 6, 7, 8, and 9 have compound subjects.

1. English settlers and Spanish settlers / came . . .
2. Trees and bushes / were . . .
3. The fierce winds and the cold temperatures / made . . .
4. The settlers and Native Americans / became . . .
5. Native Americans / helped . . .
6. Potatoes and corn / were . . .
7. English settlers and Spanish settlers / had . . .
8. Peanuts and sunflower seeds / are . . .
9. Lima beans and corn / are . . .
10. Zucchini / is . . .
11. Native Americans / also . . .

B. 1. Gold and silver from the New World were sent to Spain.
   2. France and the Netherlands staked claims in the Americas in the 1500s and 1600s.
   3. John Cabot and Henry Hudson explored areas of the Americas.

C. Discuss your answers with your instructor.

Lesson 17, Using Compound Predicates (P. 25)

A. Sentences 2, 3, 4, 6, 8, 9, 11, and 12 have compound predicates.

1. The students / organized a picnic for their families.
2. They / discussed and chose a date for the picnic.
3. They / wrote and designed invitations.
4. The invitations / were mailed and delivered promptly.

5. Twenty-five families / responded to the invitations.
6. The students / bought the food and made the sandwiches.
7. The families / bought the soft drinks.
8. The students / packed and loaded the food into a truck.
9. The families / brought and set up the volleyball nets.
10. Everyone / participated in the games and races.
11. They / ran relay races and threw water balloons.
12. Everyone / packed the food and cleaned up the picnic area at the end of the day.

B. 1. Caroline <u>heard</u> and <u>memorized</u> the music.
2. Keith <u>picked</u> up and <u>loaded</u> the newspapers into his car.
3. Larry <u>studied</u> and <u>wrote</u> down the names of the states.

C. Discuss your answers with your instructor.

Lesson 18, Simple and Compound Sentences (P. 26)

A. Sentences 1, 3, 5, and 6 are simple. Sentences 2 and 4 are compound.

1. The seven continents of the world / are North America, South America, Africa, Europe, Australia, Asia, and Antarctica.
2. Three-fourths of the earth / is covered by water, and most of it / is salty ocean water.
3. The four oceans of the world / are the Pacific, the Atlantic, the Indian, and the Arctic.
4. We / cannot exist without water, but we / cannot drink the salty ocean water.
5. Most of the water we drink / comes from lakes, rivers, and streams.
6. Clean water / is a priceless resource.

B. 1. The Pacific Ocean is the largest ocean in the world, and it covers more area than all the earth's land put together.
2. Bodies of salt water that are smaller than oceans are called seas, gulfs, or bays, and these bodies of water are often encircled by land.
3. Seas, gulfs, and bays are joined to the oceans, and they vary in size and depth.
4. The Mediterranean is one of the earth's largest seas, and it is almost entirely encircled by the southern part of Europe, the northern part of Africa, and the western part of Asia.

Lesson 19, Correcting Run-on Sentences (P. 27)

Discuss your answers with your instructor.

1. In 1860, the Pony Express started in St. Joseph, Missouri. The route began where the railroads ended.
2. People in the West wanted faster mail service. The mail took six weeks by boat.
3. Mail sent by stagecoach took about 21 days. The Pony Express averaged ten days.
4. The Pony Express used a relay system. Riders and horses were switched at 157 places along the way to Sacramento, California.
5. Because teenagers weighed less than adults, most of the riders were teenagers. The horses could run faster carrying them.
6. Riders had to cross raging rivers. The mountains were another barrier.

Lesson 20, Expanding Sentences (P. 28)

A. Discuss your answers with your instructor.

B. Discuss your answers with your instructor.

Review (P. 29)

A. 1. IN, ?
2. D, .
3. IM, .
4. X
5. D, .
6. E, !
7. IN, ?
8. X
9. E, !
10. IN, ?

B. 1. <u>You</u> / <u>must guess</u> . . .
2. <u>John</u> / <u>will write</u> . . .
3. His younger <u>sister</u> / <u>has</u> already <u>written</u> . . .
4. His twin <u>brothers</u> / <u>will write</u> . . .
5. Each <u>member</u> of the family / <u>hopes</u> . . .
6. Only one <u>person</u> / <u>can win</u>

C. 1. Maria's contest entry form came in the mail.
2. Her contestant prize number went right into the trash.
3. The winning prize number was buried in the city dump.
4. Maria will never know what she did.

Review (P. 30)

D. 1. CP
2. CS
3. R
4. C
5. CS
6. C
7. CP
8. R

E. 1. <u>Jan and Paul</u> listened to the song playing on the radio.
2. They both <u>knew the title of the song and remembered who recorded it.</u>

F. Sentences may vary. Suggested:

1. I enjoy entering recipe contests, but my favorite contests are for dessert recipes.
2. I create most of my recipes from scratch, or I add unusual ingredients to existing recipes.

G. Sentences may vary. Suggested:

1. Many people win contests every day. Some people just have to write their names on an entry form to win.
2. Some contest winners are given numbers, and the winning prize numbers are drawn randomly.

H. Discuss your answers with your instructor.

Using What You've Learned (P. 31)

A. Discuss your answers with your instructor.

B. Discuss your answers with your instructor.

C. Discuss your answers with your instructor.

D. Discuss your answers with your instructor.

Using What You've Learned (P. 32)

E. Sentences will vary. Suggested:

1. To take a good photograph, you need a good eye. You do not need an expensive camera.
2. You just load your camera and go for a walk.
3. You may see something that is different and colorful.
4. Perhaps you like the shape of an object, or maybe you like the texture.
5. Don't take your picture yet! Be sure your lens cap is off and your camera is focused correctly.
6. Think about what you do not want in your picture and the way you want to frame your picture.
7. Take your time, and keep your camera steady.

F. Discuss your answers with your instructor.

Unit 3 Grammar and Usage

Lesson 21, Nouns (P. 33)

A. Discuss your answers with your instructor.

B.
1. Alaska; gold; silver; copper; oil
2. Chocolate; beans; tree; tropics
3. distance; Texas; distance; Chicago; New York
4. men; women; horses; parade
5. city; California; San Diego
6. Alexander Graham Bell; inventor; telephone; Edinburgh, Scotland
7. Jack, Diane, plane; London; Buckingham Palace
8. animals; piranhas; alligators; anacondas; sloths; Amazon River Basin
9. tarantula; type; spider
10. Maya; people; Mexico; Central America

Lesson 22, Common and Proper Nouns (P. 34)

A. Discuss your answers with your instructor.

B. Answers will vary. Suggested:

1.	state	11.	planet
2.	continent	12.	president
3.	day	13.	month
4.	river	14.	mountains
5.	person	15.	country
6.	lake	16.	book
7.	holiday	17.	person
8.	ocean	18.	city
9.	state	19.	city
10.	person	20.	dog

Lesson 22, Common and Proper Nouns (P. 35)

C.
1. timber; oak; furniture; bridges; ships
2. painter; jeweler; farmer; engineer; inventor
3. crops; sugar; tobacco; coffee; fruits
4. groves; nuts; part
5. rivers; beaches
6. bridge; world
7. foods; lamb; fish; olives; cheese
8. road; tunnel; base; tree
9. civilizations; gold; ornaments
10. lakes
11. tree; blossoms; fruits
12. center
13. trees; turpentine; tar; resin; timber; oils
14. amount; coffee
15. pelican; penguin; flamingo; birds
16. trip; space; danger

D.
1. Brazil
2. William Penn; Pennsylvania
3. Elm Grove Library
4. Commander Byrd; North Pole
5. Dr. Jeanne Spurlock; Howard University College of Medicine
6. Europe; Asia
7. Colombia
8. Kilimanjaro; Africa
9. Navajo
10. Leticia; Carlos; Sam; Ted
11. Thomas Jefferson; United States
12. Lake Michigan
13. Quebec; North America
14. Paul Revere
15. India
16. Sears Tower; Chicago

Lesson 23, Singular and Plural Nouns (P. 36)

A.
1.	newspapers	5.	bodies
2.	guesses	6.	stories
3.	towns	7.	bushes
4.	valleys	8.	offices

9. taxes
10. toys
11. bosses
12. schools

13. days
14. copies
15. authors
16. porches

B. 1. pennies
2. dresses
3. bridges
4. brushes
5. counties

6. foxes
7. books
8. lunches
9. countries

Lesson 23, Singular and Plural Nouns (P. 37)

C. 1. knives
2. loaves
3. halves
4. mice
5. feet
6. geese

7. hooves
8. moose
9. lives
10. tomatoes
11. teeth
12. pianos

D. 1. feet
2. sheep
3. chimneys
4. cities
5. leaves

6. mosquitoes
7. nickels
8. friends
9. desks
10. benches

Lesson 24, Possessive Nouns (P. 38)

A. 1. girl's
2. child's
3. women's
4. children's
5. John's
6. baby's
7. boys'
8. teacher's

9. Dr. Ray's
10. ladies'
11. brother's
12. soldier's
13. men's
14. aunt's
15. Ms. Jones's

B. 1. Jim's cap
2. Kathy's wrench
3. baby's smile
4. friend's car
5. Kim's new shoes
6. dog's collar
7. Frank's golf clubs
8. runners' shoes
9. parents' friends
10. editor's opinion
11. children's lunches
12. Kyle's coat
13. teacher's assignment

Lesson 24, Possessive Nouns (P. 39)

C. 1. company's
2. dog's
3. women's
4. Doug's
5. David's
6. cat's
7. Kurt's

8. Men's
9. squirrel's
10. brother's
11. child's
12. calf's
13. baby's
14. teachers'

15. Alex's
16. deer's
17. Stacy's
18. country's
19. robins'
20. person's
21. sister's

22. children's
23. neighbors'
24. class's
25. boys'
26. designer's
27. horse's

Lesson 25, Appositives (P. 40)

A. The phrases in bold should be circled.

1. **my father's older brother**, Henry
2. **the Missouri Pacific**, train
3. **the location of the main station**, Seattle
4. **its main cargo**, Coal and lumber
5. **our uncle**, Henry
6. **his nephews**, us
7. **his brother**, father
8. **his sister-in-law**, mother
9. **his wife**, Aunt Emma
10. **Todd and Elizabeth**, cousins

B. Discuss your answers with your instructor.

Lesson 26, Verbs (P. 41)

1. are
2. wrote
3. Check
4. have
5. is
6. reached
7. won
8. trains
9. has
10. are
11. remember
12. bought
13. is
14. followed
15. whistled

16. watches
17. scored
18. won
19. is
20. lays
21. set
22. Answer
23. explained
24. worked
25. has
26. plays
27. Brush
28. whirled
29. arrived
30. is

Lesson 27, Verb Phrases (P. 42)

1. were held
2. invented
3. was
4. was
5. built
6. will arrive
7. was
8. has made
9. covered
10. have ridden
11. is molding
12. spent
13. are posted
14. has found
15. is going

16. have trimmed
17. exports
18. is reading
19. helped
20. was discovered
21. was called
22. are planning
23. has howled
24. have arrived
25. have written
26. can name
27. received
28. was printed
29. are working
30. was painted

Lesson 28, Helping Verbs (P. 43)

A. The words in bold should be circled.

1. **have** begun
2. **will** rake
3. **must** sweep
4. **will** pull
5. **may** prepare
6. **should** wash
7. **would** make
8. **is** working
9. **has** sprayed
10. **must** close
11. **would** enjoy
12. **might** finish

B. Discuss your answers with your instructor.

Lesson 29, More Helping Verbs (P. 44)

A. The words in bold should be circled.

1. **will be** given
2. **have been** studying
3. **may be** forming
4. **should be** reviewing
5. **Are** joining
6. **May** meet
7. **should have** known
8. **have** been
9. **have been** looking
10. **would have** met
11. **has been** delayed
12. **Would** prefer
13. **had been** enjoying
14. **have been** waiting
15. **had** been
16. **Will be** swimming
17. **must have been** splashing
18. **Could** take

B. Discuss your answers with your instructor.

C. Discuss your answers with your instructor.

Lesson 30, Using *Is/Are* and *Was/Were* (P. 45)

A.
1. Is
2. are
3. is
4. are
5. is
6. are
7. are
8. Are
9. is
10. are

B.
1. were
2. were
3. were
4. were
5. was
6. was
7. was
8. were
9. were
10. was

Lesson 31, Verb Tenses (P. 46)

A.
1. works; present
2. care; present
3. play; present
4. threw; past
5. sailed; past
6. ran; past
7. shouted; past
8. listens; present
9. got; past
10. called; past
11. went; past
12. will play; future

B.
1. My little sister followed me everywhere.
2. She came to my friend's house.
3. She rode my bicycle on the grass.

Lesson 32, Principal Parts of Verbs (P. 47)

1. is walking;   walked;   (have, has, had) walked
2. is visiting;   visited;   (have, has, had) visited
3. is watching;   watched;   (have, has, had) watched
4. is following;   followed;   (have, has, had) followed
5. is jumping;   jumped;   (have, has, had) jumped
6. is talking;   talked;   (have, has, had) talked
7. is adding;   added;   (have, has, had) added
8. is learning;   learned;   (have, has, had) learned
9. is painting;   painted;   (have, has, had) painted
10. is planting;   planted;   (have, has, had) planted
11. is working;   worked;   (have, has, had) worked
12. is dividing;   divided;   (have, has, had) divided
13. is missing;   missed;   (have, has, had) missed
14. is scoring;   scored;   (have, has, had) scored
15. is calling;   called;   (have, has, had) called
16. is collecting;   collected;   (have, has, had) collected

Lesson 33, Past Tenses of *See, Do,* and *Come* (P. 48)

1. saw
2. came
3. did
4. saw
5. did
6. came
7. done
8. come
9. seen
10. done
11. came
12. seen
13. come
14. seen
15. came
16. saw
17. did
18. come
19. saw
20. done
21. came
22. did
23. come
24. saw
25. come
26. seen
27. did
28. came
29. saw
30. done

Lesson 34, Past Tenses of *Eat* and *Drink* (P. 49)

A.
1. eaten
2. drank
3. ate
4. drunk
5. ate
6. drank
7. eaten
8. drunk
9. ate
10. drank
11. ate
12. drank
13. eaten
14. drunk
15. eaten
16. drank

B.
1. eaten
2. drank
3. ate
4. drunk

5. drank
6. eaten
7. drank
8. eaten
9. drunk
10. ate

Lesson 35, Past Tenses of *Sing* and *Ring* (P. 50)

A. 1. sung
2. rung
3. sang
4. rung
5. sang
6. rang
7. sang
8. rang
9. sung
10. rang
11. sung
12. rung
13. sang; sung
14. rung
15. sang
16. rung

B. 1. rung
2. sang
3. sung
4. rang
5. rung
6. sang
7. rang
8. sung
9. rang
10. sang

Lesson 36, Past Tenses of *Freeze, Choose, Speak,* and *Break* (P. 51)

A. 1. spoken
2. frozen
3. broke
4. spoken
5. chosen
6. broken
7. spoken
8. froze
9. chose
10. broken
11. spoke
12. froze
13. broken
14. chose
15. spoke
16. frozen

B. 1. frozen
2. broken
3. chosen
4. spoke
5. chosen
6. chose
7. broken
8. spoke
9. frozen
10. spoken

Lesson 37, Past Tenses of *Know, Grow,* and *Throw* (P. 52)

A. 1. known
2. grew
3. thrown
4. known
5. grown
6. thrown
7. grown
8. knew
9. grown
10. known
11. thrown
12. grew
13. threw
14. grown
15. knew
16. threw
17. known
18. grew

B. Discuss your answers with your instructor.

C. Discuss your answers with your instructor.

D. Discuss your answers with your instructor.

Lesson 38, Past Tenses of *Blow* and *Fly* (P. 53)

A. 1. flew
2. blown
3. flown
4. blew
5. blew
6. flown
7. flew
8. blown
9. flew
10. blown
11. flown
12. blown
13. flew
14. blown
15. flown
16. blew
17. flown
18. blew
19. flew
20. blown
21. flew
22. blew
23. flown

B. Discuss your answers with your instructor.

C. Discuss your answers with your instructor.

Lesson 39, Past Tenses of *Take* and *Write* (P. 54)

A. 1. took
2. written
3. taken
4. wrote
5. took
6. written
7. took
8. wrote
9. taken
10. written
11. took
12. written
13. took
14. wrote

B. 1. wrote
2. taken
3. written
4. taken
5. wrote
6. taken
7. wrote
8. wrote
9. took
10. wrote
11. took

Lesson 40, Past Tenses of *Give* and *Go* (P. 55)

A. 1. given
2. gone
3. gave
4. went
5. gave
6. gone
7. gave
8. gone
9. gave
10. gone
11. given
12. went
13. given
14. gone
15. given
16. gone

B. 1. went
2. given
3. gone
4. given
5. gone
6. given
7. gone
8. gave
9. went
10. given

Lesson 41, Possessive Pronouns (P. 56)

1. her
2. his
3. their
4. her
5. their
6. his
7. his
8. its
9. their
10. their
11. its
12. his
13. its
14. its
15. her
16. her
17. his
18. its
19. his
20. your

21. his   24. his
22. their   25. his
23. her   26. their

Lesson 42, Indefinite Pronouns (P. 57)

A. 1. Everyone   11. Someone
    2. somebody   12. Everybody
    3. Anything   13. Each
    4. Something   14. Some
    5. Everybody   15. Several
    6. No one   16. No one
    7. anyone   17. Everyone
    8. Both   18. Nobody
    9. Nothing   19. Everything
    10. anybody   20. anything

B. Discuss your answers with your instructor.

Lesson 43, Subject Pronouns (P. 58)

1. I   15. You
2. She   16. He
3. I   17. I
4. She   18. She
5. I   19. We
6. He   20. They
7. he   21. she
8. She; I   22. I
9. I   23. We
10. He   24. we
11. we   25. He
12. They   26. She
13. I   27. I
14. It

Lesson 44, Object Pronouns (P. 59)

1. me   15. them
2. me   16. me
3. her   17. us
4. us   18. him
5. her   19. me
6. them   20. him
7. me   21. them
8. him   22. us
9. him   23. her
10. her   24. him
11. me   25. them
12. us   26. her
13. it   27. us
14. us

Lesson 45, Subject Pronouns After Linking Verbs (P. 60)

A. 1. I   4. they
    2. she   5. she
    3. we   6. he

7. I   12. they
8. she   13. I
9. he   14. she
10. she   15. we
11. he   16. I
13. he

B. 1. they   6. he
    2. she   7. she
    3. they   8. she
    4. she   9. he
    5. they   10. she

Lesson 46, Using *Who/Whom* (P. 61)

1. Who   12. Whom
2. Who   13. Who
3. Whom   14. Who
4. Who   15. Whom
5. Who   16. Who
6. Who   17. Who
7. Whom   18. Whom
8. Whom   19. Who
9. Whom   20. Whom
10. Whom   21. Who
11. Who

Lesson 47, Using Pronouns (P. 62)

1. He; us   18. He; I
2. you   19. They; me
3. we   20. Who
4. we   21. whom; I
5. you; him   22. I; it; me
6. She; them   23. She; me
7. He; me   24. They; us
8. Who; you   25. We; he
9. I; them   26. us
10. me; she   27. you; I
11. they; us   28. You; you; it
12. I; her   29. they; us
13. you; him   30. I; them
14. you; me; I 31. us
15. her; him   32. Who
16. she; them   33. She; I; you
17. I; you   34. We; them

Lesson 48, More Pronouns (P. 63)

1. I   10. us
2. he   11. whom
3. I   12. me
4. them   13. our
5. me   14. me
6. me   15. her
7. her   16. us
8. Who   17. she
9. I   18. Who

19. their	27. Who
20. me	28. I
21. whom	29. them
22. her	30. I; his
23. us	31. whom
24. his	32. she
25. We	33. she
26. me	34. We

Lesson 49, Adjectives (P. 64)

A. Discuss your answers with your instructor.

B. Discuss your answers with your instructor.

Lesson 49, Adjectives (P. 65)

C.	1. a	26. an
	2. a	27. an
	3. a	28. a
	4. an	29. a
	5. a	30. a
	6. an	31. an
	7. a	32. an
	8. a	33. a
	9. a	34. a
	10. an	35. a
	11. an	36. a
	12. an	37. an
	13. a	38. an
	14. an	39. an
	15. a	40. a
	16. an	41. a
	17. an	42. an
	18. an	43. a
	19. an	44. an
	20. a	45. an
	21. an	46. an
	22. a	47. an
	23. an	48. a
	24. a	49. an
	25. an	50. an

Lesson 50, Proper Adjectives (P. 66)

A.	1. South American	10. Canadian
	2. African	11. Norwegian
	3. English	12. Scottish
	4. Mexican	13. Irish
	5. French	14. Chinese
	6. Russian	15. Spanish
	7. American	16. Italian
	8. Roman	17. Hawaiian
	9. Alaskan	18. Japanese

B. Discuss your answers with your instructor.

Lesson 51, Demonstrative Adjectives (P. 67)

A.	1. those	10. those
	2. these	11. those
	3. these	12. those
	4. that	13. That
	5. this	14. that
	6. Those	15. These
	7. these	16. that
	8. these	17. this
	9. those	18. This

B. Discuss your answers with your instructor.

Lesson 52, Comparing with Adjectives (P. 68)

1. smoother; smoothest
2. younger, youngest
3. sweeter; sweetest
4. stronger; strongest
5. lazier; laziest
6. greater; greatest
7. kinder, kindest
8. calmer; calmest
9. rougher; roughest
10. narrower; narrowest
11. deeper; deepest
12. shorter; shortest
13. happier; happiest
14. colder; coldest
15. prettier; prettiest

Lesson 53, More Comparing with Adjectives (P. 69)

A.
1. more energetic; most energetic
2. more courteous; most courteous
3. more impatient; most impatient
4. more important; most important
5. more difficult; most difficult
6. more wonderful; most wonderful
7. more gracious; most gracious
8. more agreeable; most agreeable

B.
1. less helpful, least helpful
2. less friendly; least friendly
3. less serious; least serious
4. less agreeable; least agreeable
5. less faithful; least faithful
6. less comfortable; least comfortable
7. less patient; least patient
8. less reliable; least reliable

Lesson 53, More Comparing with Adjectives (P. 70)

C.	1. nearer	9. youngest
	2. tallest	10. widest
	3. more helpful	11. older
	4. younger	12. largest
	5. most difficult	13. most courteous
	6. better	14. best
	7. smallest	15. coldest
	8. hottest	16. more studious

17. taller
18. wealthiest
19. fastest
20. more useful
21. most beautiful
22. narrowest

23. larger
24. best
25. worst
26. most famous
27. most beautiful

Lesson 54, Adverbs (P. 71)

A. Discuss your answers with your instructor.

B. Discuss your answers with your instructor.

Lesson 54, Adverbs (P. 72)

C.
1. slowly
2. very; quickly
3. too; early
4. patiently
5. very; cautiously
6. always; here
7. very; rapidly
8. swiftly
9. quietly; ahead
10. very; slowly
11. now
12. everywhere
13. extremely
14. always; distinctly
15. far; underwater
16. here
17. quickly
18. very; fast; especially

19. suddenly
20. softly
21. there
22. too; rapidly
23. There; extremely; very
24. politely
25. too; rapidly
26. extremely; well
27. softly
28. carefully
29. wearily
30. very; carefully
31. eagerly
32. recently
33. everywhere; yesterday
34. dearly
35. before
36. badly

Lesson 55, Comparing with Adverbs (P. 73)

1. higher; highest
2. later; latest
3. more slowly; most slowly
4. more clearly; most clearly
5. harder; hardest
6. more quickly; most quickly
7. more beautifully; most beautifully
8. longer; longest

Lesson 56, Using *Doesn't* and *Don't* (P. 74)

1. don't; doesn't
2. doesn't
3. Doesn't
4. Doesn't
5. Doesn't
6. don't
7. Doesn't
8. doesn't
9. doesn't
10. doesn't

11. don't
12. doesn't
13. doesn't
14. don't
15. doesn't
16. doesn't
17. Doesn't
18. doesn't
19. doesn't
20. doesn't

21. Don't
22. doesn't
23. doesn't
24. doesn't

25. don't
26. don't
27. Don't
28. don't

Lesson 57, Using *May/Can* and *Teach/Learn* (P. 75)

A.
1. can
2. can
3. may
4. can
5. can

6. may
7. can
8. can
9. can
10. May

B.
1. teach
2. learn
3. teach
4. learn

5. teach
6. teach
7. teach
8. teach; learn

Lesson 58, Using *Sit/Set* and *Lay/Lie* (P. 76)

A.
1. sit
2. set
3. sit
4. set
5. Set

6. sits
7. set
8. sat
9. sit
10. sit

B.
1. lay
2. Lie
3. lies
4. laid
5. lay

6. lie
7. Lay
8. laid
9. lie
10. lain

Lesson 59, Prepositions (P. 77)

1. on
2. from; with
3. through; toward
4. between
5. for
6. about
7. into
8. to
9. across
10. against
11. over; into
12. across
13. among; of
14. beside

15. across; toward
16. behind
17. around
18. on
19. about; in
20. in
21. to
22. into
23. across
24. of; from
25. among
26. After; to
27. of; in

Lesson 60, Prepositional Phrases (P. 78)

The words in bold should be circled.

1. The founders (of the **United States**) had a vision (of a great **country**).
2. We climbed (into the station **wagon**).
3. Many stars can be seen (on a clear **night**).
4. The top (of my **desk**) has been varnished.
5. Have you ever gone (through a **tunnel**)?
6. Place these memos (on the bulletin **board**).

7. We have a display (of **posters**) (in the **showcase**) (in the **corridor**).
8. Carol, take these reports (to **Ms. Garza**).
9. What is the capital (of **Alabama**)?
10. The fabric (on this antique **sofa**) came (from **France**).
11. Are you a collector (of **minerals**)?
12. I am going (to Julia's **house**).
13. The hillside was dotted (with beautiful wild **flowers**).
14. The rain beat (against the **windowpanes**).
15. We placed a horseshoe (above the **door**).
16. This poem was written (by my oldest **sister**).
17. Great clusters (of **grapes**) hung (from the **vine**).
18. Is he going (to the **race**)?
19. A herd (of **goats**) grazed (on the **hillside**).
20. Are you carrying those books (to the **storeroom**)?
21. Our car stalled (on the **bridge**).
22. My family lives (in **St. Louis**).
23. A small vase (of **flowers**) was placed (in the **center**) (of the **table**).
24. The group sat (around the **fireplace**).
25. The cold wind blew (from the **north**).
26. Doris hit the ball (over the **fence**).
27. The dog played (with the **bone**).
28. High weeds grow (by the narrow **path**).

Lesson 61, Prepositional Phrases as Adjectives/Adverbs (P. 79)

1. to the library; adverb
2. about gardening; adjective
3. in the library; adjective
4. with blue shoes; adjective
5. in the green dress; adjective
6. about the card catalog; adverb
7. for every book; adjective
8. in alphabetical order; adverb
9. in the health section; adverb
10. to the library; adjective
11. with her; adverb
12. at home; adverb
13. in the living room; adjective
14. out the window; adverb
15. by the backyard fence; adjective
16. from last year's garden; adjective
17. near the house; adverb
18. in the summer; adverb

Lesson 62, Conjunctions (P. 80)

A.
1. until
2. and
3. and
4. or
5. or
6. and
7. Neither, nor
8. but
9. and
10. for

B. Conjunctions will vary. Suggested:
1. until
2. or
3. and
4. and; but
5. until
6. and
7. and
8. if
9. and
10. Neither; nor

Lesson 63, Interjections (P. 81)

Discuss your answers with your instructor.

Review (P. 82)

A. The words in bold should be circled.

1. **John Madison** is the president of companies in **Dallas, Texas**, and **Phoenix, Arizona**.
2. **Dr. Margaret Howe** is a professor of business and economics at **Jacksonville University**.
3. Friends and relatives visiting our cabin on **Lake Erie** can enjoy swimming, fishing, boating, and hiking.

B.
1. magazines
2. flashes
3. ponies
4. potatoes
5. elves
6. stereos

C.
1. parents'
2. children's
3. teachers'
4. singers'

D.
1. seen
2. did
3. came
4. took
5. gone
6. written
7. gave
8. doesn't
9. were
10. me
11. I
12. us
13. They
14. He
15. them

Review (P. 83)

E.
1. me, our
2. I, her
3. us, them
4. We, their
5. He, she
6. Who, him
7. I, his
8. whom

F. The words in bold should be circled.

1. This, short, **comfortably,** last
2. The, large, pink
3. **many**
4. The, fastest, **easily,** the
5. **carefully,** the, complicated, the, new

G.
1. youngest
2. louder
3. most beautifully
4. faster
5. taller

H.
1. lay
2. don't
3. learn
4. can
5. sit
6. lying
7. doesn't
8. teach

I. The words in bold should be circled.

1. Put this basket (of **clothes**) (in the laundry **room**).

2. The hillside was covered (with yellow **daisies**).
3. The top (of the **mountain**) is usually covered (with **snow**).
4. The house (on the **corner**) was sold (in one **week**).

Using What You've Learned (P. 84)

B. Discuss your answers with your instructor.

C. Discuss your answers with your instructor.

D. Discuss your answers with your instructor.

E. Discuss your answers with your instructor.

F. Discuss your answers with your instructor.

G. Discuss your answers with your instructor.

Using What You've Learned (P. 85)

H. In 1585, a group of about 100 men came from England to Roanoke Island to set up a colony. They did not have enough food or supplies. The Native Americans were unfriendly. The group chose to abandon the colony. In 1586, Sir Francis Drake's fleet stopped at the colony and took the men back to England.

The English people would not give up. In 1587, three ships left England. A group of 117 men, women, and children settled on Roanoke Island. They expected to live on the supplies they received from England. In 1590, when the supply ships arrived in Roanoke, the colonists who had come in 1587 had disappeared. The people of Roanoke were never found. Their disappearance is a mystery that has never been solved.

Unit 4 **Capitalization and Punctuation**

Lesson 64, Using Capital Letters (P. 86)

A. The first letter in each of the following words should be circled and capitalized:

1. Haven't
2. The
3. Danielle; How
4. The
5. Bring
6. Who
7. The; My
8. Have

B. The first letter in each of the following words should be circled and capitalized.

1. I; I've; It; But
2. It's; Is; The; The
3. The; Children's; Hour
4. A; Wrinkle; Time
5. Stand; Me
6. Adam; Road
7. Chasing; Wind

Lesson 64, Using Capital Letters (P. 87)

C. The letters in bold should be capitalized.

chris and her friends went to a festival in **c**hicago, **i**llinois. Some of them tasted **g**reek pastry and **c**anadian cheese soup. **c**harley thought that the **i**talian sausage and **m**exican tacos were delicious! **l**aurel tried an unusual **j**apanese salad. They all watched some **i**rish folk dancers and listened to **g**erman music.

D. The first letter in each of the following words should be circled and capitalized.

1. Anita; Arizona; New; Mexico; Colorado
2. Brazil; United; States
3. Mark; Twain; Hannibal; Missouri
4. Martin; Luther; King
5. Solomon; Islands
6. North; Sea; English; Channel; Strait; Dover
7. Sam; Houston; Tennessee; Lexington; Virginia
8. St.; Augustine; United; States
9. Nairobi; Kenya
10. Japanese

Lesson 64, Using Capital Letters (P. 88)

E. The first letter in each of the following words should be circled and capitalized.

1. Captain; Cheng; Sergeant; Walters
2. Dr.; Ruth; Banks; Mr.; Juan; Gomez
3. Pres.; Alice; Slater; Mr.; Allen; Norman
4. Principal; Grissom; Mayor; Hadley
5. Halpern; Judge; Patterson
6. Mrs.; Frank; President; Howell
7. Prof.; Mary; Schneider; Dr.; David; Towne
8. Andrew; England
9. Alan; Howell; Supt.; Joyce; Randall

F. The first letter in each of the following words should be circled and capitalized.

1. Capt. Margaret K. Hansen
   2075 Lakeview St.
   Phoenix, AZ 85072
2. Jackson School Track Meet
   at Wilson Stadium
   Tues., Sept. 26, 10:30
   649 N. Clark Blvd.
3. Mr. Jonathan Bernt
   150 Telson Rd.
   Markham, Ontario L3R 1E5
4. Lt. Gary L. Louis
   5931 Congress Rd.
   Syracuse, NY 13217
5. Thanksgiving Concert
   Wed., Nov. 23, 11:00
   Practice Tues., Nov. 22, 3:30
   See Ms. Evans for details.

---

6. Gen. David Grimes
329 N. Hayes St.
Louisville, KY 40227

Lesson 65, Using End Punctuation (P. 89)

A.
1.	.	6.	?	11.	?
2.	?	7.	.	12.	.
3.	?	8.	?	13.	?
4.	.	9.	.	14.	.
5.	.	10.	?	15.	.

B.
Line 1.	?	Line 8.	.
Line 2.	?; .	Line 9.	.
Line 3.	.	Line 10.	?
Line 5.	.	Line 11.	.
Line 6.	.; ?	Line 12.	.
Line 7.	?		

Lesson 65, Using End Punctuation (P. 90)

C.
1.	.	5.	.	9.	.	13.	!
2.	!	6.	!; .	10.	!	14.	! or .
3.	!; .	7.	.	11.	! or .	15.	.
4.	.	8.	!	12.	.	16.	! or .

D.
Line 1.	.	Line 8.	! or .; ?
Line 2.	?	Line 9.	.
Line 3.	.; .	Line 10.	.; .
Line 4.	.; !	Line 11.	! or .
Line 6.	.	Line 12.	.; ?
Line 7.	.	Line 13.	. or !

Lesson 66, Using Commas (P. 91)

A.
1. The United States exports cotton, corn, and wheat to many countries.
2. The children played softball, ran races, and pitched horseshoes.
3. Lauren held the nail, and Tasha hit it with a hammer.
4. Alice, Henry, Carmen, and James go to the library often.
5. The pitcher threw a fastball, and the batter struck out.
6. Sara peeled the peaches, and Victor sliced them.
7. The mountains were covered with forests of pine, cedar, and oak.
8. Craig should stop running, or he will be out of breath.
9. Baseball is Lee's favorite sport, but Sue's favorite is football.
10. Limestone, marble, granite, and slate are found in Vermont, New Hampshire, and Maine.
11. The rain fell steadily, and the lightning flashed.
12. Mindy enjoyed the corn, but Frank preferred the string beans.

B.
1. "Please show me how this machine works," said Carolyn.
2. "Be sure you keep your eyes on the road," said the driving instructor.
3. Rick replied, "I can't believe my ears."
4. Gail said, "Travel is dangerous on the icy roads."
5. "Paul studied piano for two years," said Ms. Walters.
6. Alex said, "That goat eats everything in sight."
7. "Let's go to the park for a picnic," said Marie.
8. "Wait for me here," said Paul.
9. Tom said, "Sandra, thank you for the present."
10. "I'm going to the game with Al," remarked Frank.
11. Al asked, "What time should we leave?"
12. Chris remembered, "I was only five when we moved to New York."

Lesson 66, Using Commas (P. 92)

C.
1. Miss Hunt, do you know the answer to that question?
2. Can't you find the book I brought you last week, Roger?
3. Dr. Levin, the Smith's dentist, sees patients on weekends.
4. Oh, I guess it takes about an hour to get to Denver.
5. Joe, may Sam and I go to the ball game?
6. Our neighbor, Billy Johnson, is a carpenter.
7. What is the population of your city, Linda?
8. Well, I'm not sure of the exact number.
9. Beth, are you going skiing this weekend?
10. What time are you going to the concert, Greg?
11. Joseph, our friend, coaches the softball team.
12. Sue, have you seen a small black cat around your neighborhood?
13. Jeff, do you know Mr. D. B. Norton?
14. No, I don't think we've ever met.
15. Sally and John, would you like to go shopping on Saturday?
16. Mrs. Porter, the principal, is retiring this year.
17. Yes, the teachers are planning a retirement dinner for her.
18. Mrs. Porter and her husband, Hal, plan to move to Oregon.

D. I have two friends who are always there for me, and I tell them everything. So it was a surprise to me when Carol, my oldest friend, said, "Well, when are you moving?" I said, "What do you mean?" She said, "I don't believe you, our dearest friend, wouldn't tell us first what was going on in your life." Margie, my other friend, said, "I feel the same way. Ann, why on earth did we have to hear about this from Ray?" "Margie and Carol, I don't know what you're talking about," I said. "Oh, don't be ashamed," said Margie. "We know you must have some good reason, and we're waiting to hear it." "No, I don't have any reason because I'm not moving," I said. "Ray, that prankster, must have been trying to play a joke on us," said Carol.

Lesson 67, Using Quotation Marks and Apostrophes (P. 93)

A. 1. "Dan, did you ever play football?" asked Tim.
  2. Morris asked, "Why didn't you come in for an interview?"
  3. "I have never," said Laurie, "heard a story about a ghost."
  4. "Selina," said Yuri, "thank you for the present."
  5. "When do we start on our trip to the mountains?" asked Stan.
  6. Our guest said, "You don't know how happy I am to be in your house."
  7. "My sister," said Kelly, "bought those beautiful baskets in Mexico."
  8. "I'm going to plant the spinach," said Doris, "as soon as I get home."

B. 1. players'   4. It's   7. Men's
  2. baby's   5. captain's
  3. isn't   6. doesn't

Lesson 68, Using Colons and Hyphens (P. 94)

A. 1. 8:30   3. books: 5. Graham:
  2. Sanchez: 4. 6:15

B. 1. driving-safety, presen-   6. ear-
  2. forty-two   7. twenty-one
  3. zip-   8. air-conditioning
  4. mother-in-law   9. pup-
  5. fifty-eight

Review (P. 95)

The letters in bold should be circled and capitalized.

A. 1. Have you seen Shelly today?
  2. Is Major Bill Brandon your cousin?
  3. Mr. and Mrs. John Bell live at the Mayflower Apartments.
  4. *Alice's Adventures in Wonderland*, by Lewis Carroll, is an excellent book.
  5. How do people travel in the deserts of Egypt?
  6. *Heidi* was written by Johanna Spyri.

  7. I can't wait to spend Christmas in Florida with Uncle Will and Aunt Lee.
  8. Monticello is the beautiful home of Thomas Jefferson, near Charlottesville, Virginia.
  9. *Jungle Book* was written by Rudyard Kipling.
  10. Florida produces more oranges than any other state in the United States.
  11. "I am sure she lives at 203 Lincoln Avenue," replied Sandra.
  12. Mr. Baldwin, you won a trip to Bermuda!
  13. "The Star Spangled Banner" was written by Francis Scott Key.
  14. Mrs. Perkins has written many interesting stories about the Canadian, Alaskan, and Native American people.
  15. Isn't Mount Everest the highest mountain in the world?
  16. Have you ever crossed the Rocky Mountains?
  17. How many miles does the St. Lawrence River flow?
  18. One hundred French tourists were on the guided tour of Washington, D.C.
  19. Sometime I want to visit Mexico City.
  20. Carol R. Brink wrote a book about a boy in Scotland.
  21. The first Monday in September is known as Labor Day.
  22. The Olympic team will leave for Paris, France, on Thanksgiving Day.

Review (P. 96)

B. 1. Tom, do you know where the paper, pencils, and test forms are?
  2. "We really enjoyed our trip through Florida, Georgia, and South Carolina," said Mr. Shaw.
  3. I gave Angela, my niece, a pair of skates for her birthday, and her parents gave her a radio.
  4. "Jason, please wash, dry, and fold the laundry for me," said Connie.
  5. Dr. Wells, our family doctor, is retiring, but Dr. Hernandez will take over her practice.
  6. Yes, I think Ms. Lawson, my supervisor, is a courteous, capable, and fair person.
  7. I want to go to the beach on our vacation, but my friend wants to go camping, hiking, and fishing.
  8. Do you want to go to a movie or play cards, Sharonda?
  9. Mr. Coe, my English instructor, said, "Make sure your reports are neat, concise, and accurate."
  10. Dawn told Ms. Mendez, a nurse, about Kelsey's fever.

11. James will mow the yard, trim the hedge, and water the flowers.

12. Sara Powell, the district attorney, will look into the case.

C. 1. My mother-in-law said, "Mary's aunt will join us for dinner at 7:30."

2. Rosa couldn't find the following items for her trip: suntan lotion, her hat, and the keys to the cabin.

3. "Juan," asked Linda, "will you please bring forty-eight cookies for the club's bake sale?"

4. Ms. Tyson's secretary began the letter with "Dear Sir: I am writing on behalf of Ms. Tyson."

5. Scott said, "I'm going to Jim's house tonight at 8:00 to help him finish his son's desk."

6. Meg's friends gave her many gifts at her good-bye party: a new shirt, two headbands, stationery, and a roll of stamps.

7. "Mike and Todd don't have to go to bed until 9:30," said Larry.

8. Mr. Reid's son is only twenty-one years old and is already a well-known figure in the com-munity.

9. Rita said, "The beautiful memorial fountain is near the park's main entrance."

10. "Won't you be taking the coach's extra-credit class?" asked Eric.

11. Stephanie's party begins at 8:30.

12. "What time is your appointment, Jack?" asked Diane.

13. Today is her father's fifty-seventh birthday.

14. I thought I'd pick you up at 6:30, since we don't have to be there until 7:00.

15. Jody's father-in-law owns a chain of stores that sell men's clothing.

Using What You've Learned (P. 97)

A. The letters in bold should be circled.

one of **a**esop's fables is called "**t**he **f**ox and the **c**row." **i**t tells about a crow that stole a piece of cheese. **t**he crow landed on the branch of a tree, put the cheese in her mouth, and began to eat it. **b**ut a fox was also interested in the cheese. **h**e sat under the branch, and he thought about eating the cheese, too.

the fox said, "**c**row, **i** compliment you on your size, beauty, and strength. **y**ou would be the queen of all birds if you had a voice."

"**c**aw!" exclaimed the crow.

well, the crow dropped the cheese. **t**he fox pounced on it, carried it off a few feet, and then turned around.

"**m**y friend," said the fox, "you have every good quality except common sense."

our neighbor, **d**enise **b**aldwin, likes to tell me funny stories. **o**ne hot **f**riday afternoon in **a**ugust she told me about her trip to **a**tlanta, **g**eorgia. **s**he was walking out of a store with some presents she had bought for **p**at, her sister. **t**hey were three joke gifts which included the following: birthday candles that didn't blow out, a silly hat, and a mustache attached to some glasses. **d**enise accidentally bumped into another shopper.

"**i**'m so sorry!" exclaimed **d**enise.

"**a**re you hurt?" asked the other shopper.

"**n**o, **i**'m not hurt," said **d**enise. **b**oth shoppers had dropped their presents, and they bent over to pick them up.

"**i**'m **d**enise **b**aldwin," she said as she picked up the presents.

"**m**y name is **c**arol **s**chwartz," said the other shopper.

both shoppers said they were sorry again and then went on their way.

denise gave her sister the presents when she returned to **m**iami, **f**lorida. **p**at had a puzzled look on her face when she unwrapped them. **t**he packages contained a rattle, a bib, and a baby bonnet!

"**o**h!" gasped **d**enise. "**i** must have picked up the wrong presents when **i** bumped into **m**s.**s**chwartz."

"**w**ho's **m**s. **s**chwartz?" asked **p**at.

denise laughed and said, "**i** hope she's someone who likes joke gifts!"

Using What You've Learned (P. 98)

B. Sir Walter Scott, one of the world's greatest storytellers, was born in Edinburgh, Scotland, on August 15, 1771. Walter had an illness just before he was two years old that left him lame for the rest of his life. His par-ents were worried, so they sent him to his grandparents' farm in Sandy Knowe. They thought the country air would do him good.

Walter's parents were right. He was quite healthy by the time he was six years old. He was happy, too. Walter loved listening to his grandfather tell stories about Scotland. The stories stirred his imagination. He began to read fairy tales, travel books, and history books. It was these ear-ly stories that laid the groundwork for Scott's later interest in writing stories. His most famous book, *Ivanhoe,* has been read by people around the world.

Lesson 76, Revising and Proofreading (P. 106)

A.   Yellowstone National Park is the oldest and largest national park in the United States. It is located partly in northwestern Wyoming, partly in southern Montana, and partly in eastern Idaho. During the summer of 1988, large parts of the park were damaged by fire. A serious lack of rain was part of the reason the fire was so severe. One fire threatened to destroy the park's famous lodge, which is constructed entirely of wood. Fortunately, firefighters' efforts saved the lodge from destruction. Today the forests are slowly recovering from the fires.

Lesson 76, Revising and Proofreading (P. 107)

B. although yellowstons national park is the largest ~~national~~ national park in the United states, other national parks are also well-known yosemite national park in california has acres of Mountain Scenery and miles of hiking trails. Won of the world's largest ~~biggest~~ waterfalls can also be found in yosemite.

mammoth cave national park in kentucky features a huge underground cave the cave over has 212 miles of corridors it also ~~have~~ has underground lakes rivers and waterfalls this cave system is estimated to be millions of years old

many pepul are surprized to learn that their are national parks in alaska and hawaii. mount McKinley the highest mountain in north america is located in denali national park in alaska. you can travel to hawaii and visit hawaii volcanoes national park this Park Has too active volcanoes rare plants and animals.

   Although Yellowstone National Park is the largest national park in the United States, other national parks are also well-known. Yosemite National Park in California has acres of mountain scenery and miles of hiking trails. One of the world's largest waterfalls can also be found in Yosemite.

   Mammoth Cave National Park in Kentucky features a huge underground cave. The cave has over 212 miles of corridors. It also has underground lakes, rivers, and waterfalls. This cave system is estimated to be millions of years old.

   Many people are surprised to learn that there are national parks in Alaska and Hawaii. Mount McKinley, the highest mountain in North America, is located in Denali National Park in Alaska. You can travel to Hawaii and visit Hawaii Volcanoes National Park. This park has two active volcanoes, rare plants, and animals.

Lesson 77, Writing a Business Letter (P. 108)

A. 1. Chris Morrow
   2. Dear Sir or Madam:
   3. 9940 Main Street, Brooklyn, NY 11227
   4. April 4, 1994

Lesson 77, Writing a Business Letter (P. 109)

B. Discuss your answers with your instructor. The addresses should be circled.

Review (P. 110)

A. Discuss your answers with your instructor.

B. Discuss your answers with your instructor.

C. Discuss your answers with your instructor.

D. 1. a, c   **2.** a, b   **3.** a, c

Review (P. 111)

E. Discuss your answers with your instructor.

F. Flying a kite can be fun, but it can also serve some practical purposes. For example, Benjamin franklin uses a kite in his experiments with electricity. In the early part of the twentieth century, box kites carring instruments measured wind speed, temperature, pressure, and and humidity. they were also used to lift soldiers to hieghts where they could see the enemy. Today they serve as signals in air-see-rescue operations.

G. 1. heading
   2. inside address
   3. greeting
   4. body
   5. closing
   6. signature

Using What You've Learned (P. 112)

A. Discuss your answers with your instructor.

Using What You've Learned (P. 113)

B. Discuss your answers with your instructor.

Unit 6 Study Skills

Lesson 78, Dictionary: Guide Words (P. 114)

A. The following words should be checked:
   1. fruit
      furnish
      gate
      gallon
      fuzz
      galaxy
      future
   2. muddy
      moss
      motorcycle
      moose
      morning
      mortal
   3. perfume
      pick
      photo
      pest
      pillow
      pile

B. The words should be numbered as follows:

1. rabbit / remind	2. scent / silent	3. occasion / only
2	3	2
3	8	9
1	9	5
5	11	6
7	12	8
9	1	4
8	10	10
4	7	7
11	6	3
12	4	11
10	2	1
6	5	12

Lesson 79, Dictionary: Syllables (P. 115)

A. 1. advertise   **5.** concrete
   2. blunder   **6.** microphone
   3. paradise   **7.** incident
   4. mischievous   **8.** value

B. 1. bi-cy-cle   **8.** the-o-ry
   2. so-lu-tion   **9.** won-der-ful
   3. cat-e-go-ry   **10.** bi-ol-o-gy
   4. pun-ish-ment   **11.** siz-zle
   5. be-hav-ior   **12.** for-eign
   6. quar-ter-back   **13.** trans-par-ent
   7. dis-ap-pear   **14.** civ-i-li-za-tion

C. 1. mos-quito   mosqui-to
   2. am-bition   ambi-tion

---

3. bound-ary   bounda-ry
4. ginger-bread   gin-gerbread
5. Answers will vary.
6. leader-ship   lead-ership

Lesson 80, Dictionary: Pronunciation (P. 116)

A. 1. at
2. 5
3. Discuss your answers with your instructor.
4. hw
5. rüle
6. th

B. 1. alive   9. supper
2. load   10. locker
3. true   11. home
4. thick   12. fought
5. fallen   13. might
6. cape   14. fool
7. ice   15. freeze
8. they   16. lettuce

Lesson 81, Dictionary: Definitions and Parts of Speech (P. 117)

1. speckle
2. specify
3. specimen
4. spectacular
5. Discuss your answers with your instructor.
6. Discuss your answers with your instructor.
7. Discuss your answers with your instructor.
8. Discuss your answers with your instructor.
9. spectacular
10. specimen

Lesson 82, Dictionary: Word Origins (P. 118)

1. wampum   9. utter
2. strings of money   10. taxes
3. pasteurize   11. utter
4. chaise longue   12. out
5. chair; long   13. field
6. gardenia   14. gardenia
7. wampum   15. chaise longue
8. campus, gardenia

Lesson 83, Using Parts of a Book (P. 119)

A. 1. copyright page
2. index
3. title page
4. table of contents

B. 1. 1995
2. Steck-Vaughn Company
3. Austin, TX
4. 114
5. 33

6. Lesson 74, Outlining
7. 3, 34, 35, 66, 86–88, 95, 97, 98, 138, 146
8. 2, 57, 145
9. Lesson 2, Homonyms
10. Vocabulary
11. Possessive Nouns
12. 18
13. Study Skills
14. 110
15. Past Tenses of *Blow* and *Fly*

Lesson 84, Using the Library (P. 120)

A. 1. 600–699   9. 700–799
2. 400–499   10. 300–399
3. 000–099   11. 400–499
4. 900–999   12. 500–599
5. 100–199   13. 600–699
6. 200–299   14. 800–899
7. 500–599   15. 900–999
8. 800–899

B. Discuss your answers with your instructor.

Lesson 85, Using the Card Catalog (P. 121)

A. 1. Hoobler, Dorothy and Thomas
2. Images across the ages: African portraits
3. 96
4. 920.067   H66
5. 1993
6. African history

B. 1. subject   4. subject
2. title   5. author
3. author   6. title

Lesson 86, Using an Encyclopedia (P. 122)

1. Clarence Birdseye
2. 1886–1956
3. Amherst College
4. developing methods of preserving foods, and marketing quick-frozen foods
5. lighting technology, wood-pulping methods, and heating processes
6. food processing
7. Discuss your answers with your instructor.
8. no

Lesson 87, Finding an Encyclopedia Article (P. 123)

A. 1. 3   9. 14
2. 14   10. 17
3. 19   11. 3
4. 16   12. 19
5. 14   13. 9
6. 11   14. 6
7. 11   15. 15
8. 7

B. Discuss your answers with your instructor.

C. Discuss your answers with your instructor.

Lesson 88, Using Visual Aids (P. 124)

1. Terry
2. Julia, Miguel and Terry
3. Miguel
4. Ted
5. graph
6. chart

Lesson 88, Using Visual Aids (P. 125)

1. south
2. Walnut Street and Oak Street
3. school
4. Riverside Drive
5. Pine Street,
6. north
7. north and south
8. about 7 miles, or 11 kilometers

Lesson 89, Using a Thesaurus (P. 126)

A. 1. heat
2. warmth, fire, flame, fever, emotion, glow, blush, redness
3. flame
4. fever
5. cold, coolness, ice, chilliness
6. coolness, chilliness
7. cold

B. 1. fire
2. warmth
3. glow
4. redness
5. fever
6. flame
7. blush
8. emotion

Lesson 90, Choosing Reference Sources (P. 127)

1. dictionary
2. dictionary, encyclopedia, or atlas
3. encyclopedia
4. atlas
5. encyclopedia
6. encyclopedia
7. dictionary
8. dictionary
9. encyclopedia
10. encyclopedia or atlas
11. encyclopedia
12. dictionary
13. encyclopedia or atlas
14. encyclopedia
15. encyclopedia or atlas
16. encyclopedia
17. dictionary
18. encyclopedia or atlas
19. dictionary
20. encyclopedia

Review (P. 128)

A. 1. noun
2. 1
3. 2
4. twin
5. tuxedo
6. 3; 1
7. noun, adjective, verb
8. c. tusk/twirl

B. 1. table of contents
2. title page
3. copyright page
4. index

C. 1. by call numbers
2. author, title, subject
3. author card

Review (P. 129)

D. 1. New; countries
2. South; states
3. palm; trees

E. 1. west
2. about 4 miles, or 5 kilometers
3. north

F. 1. sweet
2. pleasant, pure, fresh, sugary
3. pleasant

G. 1. dictionary
2. atlas or encyclopedia
3. encyclopedia

Using What You've Learned (P. 130)

A. Discuss your answers with your instructor.

B. Discuss your answers with your instructor.

C. 1. b (subject card)
2. Fiona MacDonald
3. New view: Rain forest
4. Raintree/Steck-Vaughn
5. yes
6. 574.5 M235

Using What You've Learned (P. 131)

D. 1. Discuss your answers with your instructor.
2. Discuss your answers with your instructor.
3. Discuss your answers with your instructor.

E. 1. Jeff and Lupe
2. Steve
3. Lupe
4. chart

 Final Reviews

Final Review, Unit 1 (P. 132)

1. A
2. S
3. S
4. S
5. A
6. S

7. A   12. A
8. S   13. S
9. A   14. S
10. S   15. S
11. A

1. stakes
2. meet
3. bore
4. needs
5. bread
6. son
7. plane
8. hear

Discuss your answers with your instructor.

Final Review, Unit 1 (P. 133)

1. impossible
2. successful
3. rewrite
4. uncertain

1. Where is; air/plane
2. it is; down/town
3. Is not; head/quarters
4. they are; high/rise

1. homely
2. old
3. raved
4. fascinating

Discuss your answers with your instructor.

1. hit the sack
2. left high and dry
3. up in the air
4. all thumbs

Final Review, Unit 2 (P. 134)

1. E; ! or D; .   5. X   9. X
2. IN;?   6. D; .   10. E; ! or D; .
3. X   7. IM; . 11. E; !
4. IN; ?   8. IN; ? 12. D; .

Sentence 8 should be circled.

1. Bicycling / is . . .
2. Cyclists / can learn . . .
3. cyclists / wear . . .
4. helmet / is . . .
5. Experts / recommend . . .
6. riders / should learn . . .
7. people. . . / should obey. . .
8. Are / you . . .

1. CP, John Scott / is . . .
2. CS, His wife and two children / ride . . .
3. CS, John and his wife / run . . .

4. CP, The Scott children / visit . . .
5. CP, The Scott family / helps . . .
6. CS, Victoria and Nick Scott / think . . .

Final Review, Unit 2 (P. 135)

1. A bicycle safety course is offered at our neighborhood center, and the class is for children and adults together.
2. People are taught important traffic rules, and they learn ways to prevent bicycle thefts.
3. Everyone must pass a final bicycling test, because they will not get a certificate if they fail.

Final Review, Unit 3 (P. 136)

1. n., v., pp.
2. adj., n., adv.
3. int., adj., adv.
4. conj., pron., v., pp.
5. pp., v., pron., n., prep.
6. n., adj., n., pp.
7. pron., v., adj., n.
8. adj., pron., adj., adj.

1. were   9. sung
2. completed 10. chosen
3. seen   11. broken
4. came   12. grew
5. done   13. gone
6. drank   14. given
7. eaten   15. written
8. rang

Final Review, Unit 3 (P. 137)

Answers will vary. Sample paragraphs follow:

  Trees are important for their products and their benefits to the environment. Wood is one of the main building supplies in the world and an important fuel. Paper and paper products are made from wood pulp. Trees also produce various nuts and fruits for both animals and humans.

  One way trees help the environment is by releasing oxygen into the air. For instance, if a tree has taken in sunlight and carbon dioxide, it will release oxygen. Tree roots help control erosion and flooding. Trees have always given homes for shelter for many animals. Raccoons, squirrels, and other animals make their homes in trees.

Many trees have lived and grown for thousands of years and are hundreds of feet tall. The redwoods in California are some of the tallest trees in the world. The tallest tree is 364 feet tall and lives in Humboldt National Forest. The oldest living tree is a bristlecone pine in Nevada that is over 4,600 years old.

Final Review, Unit 4 (P. 138)

The first letter in each of the following words should be circled and capitalized. End punctuation should also be added.

1. How; ?; Marie
2. Her; .
3. It's; ! ; Peter
4. Marie; Peter; George; .
5. I; George; .
6. I'd; Marie; .
7. Then; ?; Peter;
8. Marie; .
9. That's; !
10. Peter; George; Marie; .

122 E. Park Street
Denver, CO 81442
October 10, 1994

Mr. Marshall Chase
3910 Prairie Avenue
Lowell, MA 01740

Dear Mr. Chase:

Thank you very much for your interest in my star-gazing book, *A Guide to the Stars.* I published it in September through a well-known astronomy publisher, The Sky's the Limit Press. According to my publisher, books will be available at bookstores this month.

I have the answer to your question on how I do my research. I have a very powerful telescope that I use every day. I do most of my work at night between 10:15 P.M. and 1:30 A.M. I find those to be the darkest hours out here in Colorado. Finally, I have a piece of advice for budding astronomers. Always keep a journal of the stars you see each night, and try to memorize their location. I always say to my students, "The sky's the limit!" Good luck star-gazing.

Sincerely,
Professor Liz Nelson

Final Review, Unit 4 (P. 139)

Ted Carter, a United Nations spokesperson, announced, "Many remote towns and villages in Mexico have been destroyed by a major earthquake, and the United States and Canada are sending emergency relief. International troops will help with fires, flooding, and injuries resulting from the earthquake." The spokesperson further stated, "Colonel Marks, commander of relief troops, will oversee medical staff, rescue crews, and cleanup operations." Mr. Carter said, "The troops will provide medical supplies, food, water, and temporary shelter for the earthquake victims." He ended his statement by saying, "The troops are preparing now, and they should begin arriving in Mexico tomorrow morning." Mr. Carter then told the reporters that he would answer some questions.

"Mr. Carter, are any more countries involved in the relief efforts?" asked Dorian Kramer, reporter for the *Richland Register.*

Mr. Carter replied, "Yes. England, France, and Germany are also sending supplies and medical staff."

Pete Simmons, KRSS reporter, asked, "How long will our troops be in Mexico?"

Mr. Carter responded, "Well, the President is not sure, but we expect the troops to be there several weeks."

Joe Kelly, *Up-Date* magazine reporter, asked, "How many deaths and injuries have been reported?"

"We do not have exact figures, but we know there are many people hurt and missing," said Mr. Carter.

1. The boys' father didn't want them to stay home alone.
2. Of all the countries I've visited, these countries' scenery impressed me most: England, France, and Switzerland.
3. The flowers' petals weren't as colorful as the pictures showed them to be.
4. The Los Angeles mayor's speeches at the national mayors' convention will be at these times: 5:00 P.M., 7:30 P.M., and 9:00 P.M.
5. My house's roof wasn't damaged by hail, but other houses' roofs were: Jim's roof, my father-in-law's roof, my cousin's roof, and Ms. Brown's roof.
6. Many children attend our public library's children's hour on Tuesdays from 9:00 A.M. to 10:00 A.M.
7. The new store's advertisement said it specializes in men's and women's clothing, ladies' jew-elry, and perfumes from around the world.
8. The winner's trophy will be awarded to one out of the twenty-two contestants.

Final Review, Unit 5 (P. 140)

Discuss your answers with your instructor.

1. a, b
2. a, c
3. b, c

Final Review, Unit 5 (P. 141)

Did you know that roughly three-quarters of the earth's fresh water is not held in rivers and lakes? The water is held in glaciers, large sheets of ice that form in high altitudes and polar regions such as Antarctica and Greenland. There are between 70,000 and 200,000 glaciers in the world.

As temperatures warm, glaciers melt a little and move at a rate that can't be seen. As they move, they sometimes freeze and add to their mass before moving on. They actually reshape the land they pass over. The most famous glaciers are in Europe. The best-known ones are in the French and Swiss Alps.

Final Review, Unit 6 (P. 142)

1. c. (fire / flight)
2. 3; 2
3. noun
4. 1
5. (flēt); (furm)
6. firm

1. table of contents
2. index
3. copyright page
4. title page

1. atlas or encyclopedia
2. dictionary
3. encyclopedia
4. thesaurus or dictionary
5. atlas or encyclopedia
6. encyclopedia
7. dictionary or thesaurus
8. dictionary

Final Review, Unit 6 (P. 143)

1. Philip Arthur Sauvain
2. 302.2   S28
3. 1990
4. Raintree/Steck-Vaughn

1. Tuesday and Thursday
2. Friday
3. Wednesday
4. graph

Check What You've Learned (P. 144)

A. 1. H   **3.** A
2. S   **4.** H

B. smart

C. 1. C   **3.** P
2. S   **4.** S

D. 1. they have
2. we would

E. clever

F. a

G. The words in bold should be circled.

  1. IM, **(You)**, make
  2. IN, **you**, are feeling
  3. E, **That**, hurts
  4. D, **I**, will be

H. 1. CS
  2. CP

I. 1. I
  2. CS
  3. RO

J. The words in bold should be circled.

The newspaper told about the departure of **Juan Carlos** from the country of **Chile**.

Check What You've Learned (P. 145)

K. Maria's

L. The word in bold should be circled.
It was the new **visitor**, Kevin, who had the most interesting ideas.

M. The word in bold should be circled.
He **is** still having doubts about his dinner party.

N. 1. future
  2. past
  3. present

O. 1. drink, frozen
  2. went, flew
  3. broke, threw

P. The words in bold should be circled.

  1. IP, **Everyone**
  2. SP, **He**
  3. OP, **her**
  4. PP, **Their**

Q. 1. adverb
  2. adverb
  3. adjective
  4. adjective

R. 1. may   **4.** lain
  2. sit   **5.** doesn't
  3. teach

S. The words in bold should be circled.
I think we will find the solution **to** the problem, and everyone will agree **on** it.

Check What You've Learned (P. 146)

T.
733 W. Martin
Paducah, KY 55809
Mar. 13, 1994

Dear Ms. Simpson:
  Please send me twenty-one copies of the pamphlet "Don't Ever Stop Trying." My students will enjoy its positive message. I've enclosed an addressed and stamped envelope for your convenience. Thank you.

Yours truly,
Leslie Stone

U. Discuss your answers with your instructor.

V. **1.** 1   **4.** 4
   2. 2   **5.** 3
   3. 5   **6.** 6

W. outline

Check What You've Learned (P. 147)

X. **1.** noun   **4.** 1
   2. after   **5.** complaint
   3. harp / hate   **6.** har-vest

Y. where a chapter begins

Z. **1.** card catalog
   2. dictionary
   3. atlas or encyclopedia
   4. encyclopedia
   5. atlas